ELEMENTARY SPANISH CHATBOOK

chat•book (*chat-bŭk*) —*noun*
A conversational workbook with Spanish lessons for K-6 students

BY

JULIE JAHDE POSPISHIL

WITH CARTOONS BY SONIA CARBONELL

www.SpanishChatCompany.com
Omaha, Nebraska

Revised Edition: February 2018

Copyright @ 2013 by Spanish Chat Company

All rights reserved. No part of this book may be reproduced or transmitted in any form or by any means, electronic or mechanical, including photocopying, recording, or by any information storage and retrieval system, without permission in writing from the publisher. The author acknowledges that there are many differences in language translation and have attempted to select a form of Spanish that will be understood in the vast majority of Spanish-speaking situations. For more information and to contact the authors go to: www.SpanishChatCompany.com.

ISBN 13: 978-0-9824625-9-1

LCCN: 2013908126

Library of Congress Cataloging-in Publication Data on file with publisher.

Published by: Spanish Chat Company
       www.SpanishChatCompany.com
Visit our website for Spanish Chatshow movies, CD's and learning opportunities

Printed in the United States of America

10 9 8 7 6 5 4 3 2 1

ELEMENTARY SPANISH CHATBOOK IS GETTING RAVE REVIEWS:

The Spanish Chatbook activities combine lessons on language, history and culture, all wrapped up in an energetic, dynamic presentation. As a principal at a Dual Language school, I have found the Spanish Chatbook classes have helped me communicate more effectively with my students and families. Maestra Julia makes learning Spanish interesting, engaging and fun! I highly recommend Spanish Chatbook for everyone!

—Marjorie Schmid, Principal,
Crestridge Elementary International Studies &
Dual Language Magnet Center

"It's just so much fun!! It is awesome! We get to make fun art and try new foods!"

—Connor, 4th grade

"Maestra Julia's activities have made Spanish learning fun for my daughter! She is able to teach the children not just the language, but much about the different Spanish cultures as well!"

—Maria Michaelis, M.D.
Mother of Elementary Spanish Student

CHEERS FOR THE SPANISH CHATBOOKS:

This was the best Spanish learning experience I ever had. The class was extremely upbeat and fun."

—Tess Snyder
Woodmen of the World Insurance Agency

"As a tenured educator and facilitator I truly appreciated Julie's ability to flexibly adapt to multiple learning styles in her training/classroom. Two years of studying Spanish was nothing compared to what I learned in two weeks time with Julie. Her philosophy works!"

—Spencer K. Terry, Private Consultant

"When learning to speak a new language, students often feel shy or intimidated when trying to put together more than a few words. Spanish Chat Company's method of teaching Spanish makes the learning process fun and easy, so students show more confidence in pronouncing words and forming sentences. I would recommend these beneficial key words and phrases — whether for personal or business use."

—Deb Barelos, Circulation Manager
Omaha Public Library

PRAISE FOR ANOTHER GREAT BOOK BUSINESS SPANISH CHATBOOK:

"The practical and enjoyable lessons were designed to teach our employees to communicate with our Spanish-speaking customers. We learned the language, plus important cultural facts about Spanish-speaking countries."

—Pat Tooles, Corporate Performance
Omaha Public Power District

"I have really enjoyed the *Business Spanish Chatbook*. The pronunciation guides and phrases are valuable tools that I use often in my day-to-day work."

—Jill Regester, Communications Manager
Woodmen of the World Insurance Agency

"The lessons are easy to follow and understand, and the phrases we learned were exactly what we needed to better serve our customers. Julie has that rare gift of making learning fun. She brings such exuberance to her classes, the students learn easily."

—Terry Wingate, Volunteer Coordinator
Omaha Public Library

"Spanish Chatbook is an experience of enthusiasm for the topic. Julie is pragmatic, able to teach at the appropriate level, yet challenging in a polite way."

—Dr. Charles Filipi, Professor of Surgery
Creighton University

HERE IS WHAT PEOPLE ARE SAYING ABOUT CULINARY SPANISH CHATBOOK:

"Welcome to the way you will learn Spanish. This is the perspective that should be taken with all languages. Gracias Maestra!"

—Phil Nicols, Culinary student

"Maestra Julia is an engaged and dynamic instructor in the classroom whose passion para el Español y la cocina has also permeated this project."

—Chef Brian O'Malley Academic Director
Institute for the Culinary Arts
Metropolitan Community College

"Culinary Spanish Chatbook is a 'must have' for everyone working in the food industry. There is nothing more frustrating than not being able to communicate with a co-worker. This book is a great tool to break down those barriers, and it's realistic, upbeat approach makes learning Spanish fun."

—Karen Popp, Operations Manager
WheatFields Eatery and Bakery

WANT TO LEARN SPANISH OR ENGLISH?

Would you like to order more books for coworkers, friends or family?
Here is how: Order online at SpanishChatCompany.com

ONLINE GAMES, FLASHCARDS, ACTIVITIES & VIDEOS

SPANISHCHATCOMPANY.COM

MINI CHATBOOKS

ABOUT THE AUTHOR

Julie Jahde Pospishil studied for a semester at the University in San Sebastian, Spain, and has an M.A. in Education-Language Acquisition from the University of Nebraska–Omaha. She has an undergraduate degree in Elementary Education with an emphasis on Spanish. Julie has directed a Spanish summer camp for eight summers where each day elementary students participated in cooking new recipes and creating art projects while immersed in Spanish. Julie has taught Spanish for 20 years in elementary schools in Nebraska, Iowa and Texas, and she has worked for a grant through the U.S. Department of Education to produce ten Spanish language videos for children in addition to training elementary school teachers to speak Spanish and communicate with Hispanic families.

Julie customizes Adult Spanish Classes for Omaha Public Schools, Boystown Pediatrics–Bergan Mercy Hospital, Omaha Public Power District (OPPD), Omaha Public Libraries, Dana College, Woodmen of the World, Casinos, communications companies, First Data Resources, many banks and Metropolitan Community College. She and her husband, Brad, own Spanish Chat Company, and love traveling together. They have spent time in 16 different Latin American countries, meeting many amigos. Brad enjoys these "Aventuras con Julia."

Julie currently teaches *Spanish Chatbook 1, Spanish Chatbook 2, Business Spanish Chatbook, Elementary English Chatbook and Culinary Spanish Chatbook* classes. In 2013, Julie produced an audio CD for Latina breast cancer survivors called, *"Un Tiempo para Sanar."* Julie enjoys cooking Latin American dishes with her children, Jaden and Elena. Her children spend half of their day learning in Spanish in the dual language program at their International Studies magnet public school. She believes "everyone smiles in the same language" and "donde existe voluntad, siempre hay un camino. = Where there's a will, there's a way."

POSITIVE AFFIRMATIONS

PICK 3 OF THESE THAT DESCRIBE YOU. USE A NEW PHRASE EACH DAY!
FIND THE SPANISH ONLY CHART ON PAGE 120.

BE KIND! GIVE A COMPLIMENT!
¡Bien hecho! = Well done!
¡Brilliante! = Brilliant!
¡Buen trabajo! = Good work!
¡Espectacular! = Spectacular!
¡Estupendo/a! = Wonderful!
¡Excelente! = Excellent!
Excepcional! = Exceptional
¡Extraordinario/a! = Extraordinary!
¡Fabuloso/a! = Fabulous!
¡Fantástico/a! = Fantastic!
¡Fenomenal! = Phenomenal!
¡Genial! = Clever!
¡Impresionante! = Impressive!
¡Increíble! = Incredible!
¡Magnífico/a! = Magnificent
¡Marvilloso/a! = Marvelous
¡Muy bien! = Very good!
¡Perfecto/a! = Perfect!
¡Qué bien! = Great!
¡Qué chévere! = Cool!
¡Ideal! = Great!
¡Sobresaliente! = Outstanding!
¡Sensacional! = Sensational!
¡Super! = Super!
¡Superior! = Superior!

YO SOY...TU ERES...ELLA ES...ÉL ES... I AM...YOU ARE...SHE IS...HE IS...
admirable = admirable
amable = friendly
asombroso / asombrosa = amazing
atlético/a = athletic
bonito/a = cute / pretty / beautiful
bueno / buena = good
cortés = courteous
especial = special
exitoso / exitosa = successful
fascinante = fascinating
inteligente = intelligent
listo / lista = smart
organizado/a = organized
paciente = patient
precioso/a = precious / beautiful
puntual = punctual
respetuoso/a = respectful
responsable = responsible
simpático/a = nice
un buen amigo / una buena amiga = a good friend
un buen estudiante / una buena estudiante = a good student
un ganador / una ganadora = a winner
un trabajador / una trabajadora = hard worker
único / única = unique
valiente = brave

INTRODUCTION / INTRODUCCIÓN

ELEMENTARY SPANISH CHATBOOK

EN CADA LECCIÓN = IN EACH LESSON:

 **¡Repítelo! = Repeat it!** (Vocabulary)

 ¡Cántalo! = Sing it! (Song)

 **¡Inténtalo! = Try it!** (Group game)

 **¡Léelo! = Read it!** (Spanish flashcards)

¡Practícalo! = Practice it! (English version)

 ¡Juégalo! = Play it! (Game)

 ¡Míralo! = Look at it! (Culture)

 **¡Hazlo! = Do it!** (Art)

 **¡Cocínalo! = Cook it!** (Recipe)

 ¡Termínalo! = Finish it! (Homework)

BIENVENIDOS = WELCOME

QUERIDOS MAESTROS Y PADRES = DEAR TEACHERS AND PARENTS

NECESITA = YOU WILL NEED:

- **Tijeras =** Scissors

- **Sobre =** Envelope for flashcards

- **Dados =** Dice - You need one pair of dice for every 3 students.

- **Instrumentos =** Instruments or maracas per person or at least one maraca for the class for the game in Lesson 1.

- **Frijoles =** Beans for bingo or you can use small squares cut from paper.

- **Ingredientes =** Ingredients to make the recipes.

- **Materiales =** Materials to make the crafts. The recipes and crafts will let you know the exact materials.

- **Libros** = Books - *Elementary Spanish Chatbook*: One book per student.

- **Audio** = *Elementary Spanish Chatbook Song CD* - One CD or online access for the musical songs to enhance learning.

- **Online Access or Spanish Chatshow DVD's:** Videos with kids cooking or with Sign language for all the vocabulary in this *Elementary Spanish Chatbook*. Use the videos to reinforce your lessons. Find more information at SpanishChatCompany.com

TABLE OF CONTENTS & INTRODUCTION 1
   Notas = Notes About The *Elementary Spanish Chatbook* for Adults 4
   Group Classroom Commands (English First) 5
   Audio Track Listing 6
   Lección: Verbos, Temas & Cultura = Lesson: Verbs, Themes $ Culture 7
   Nombre = Name: A Spanish Name List 8
   Make Your Own Nametag 9

LESSON 1: ¿CÓMO TE LLAMAS? = WHAT IS YOUR NAME?
   ¡Repítelo! = Repeat it! Nuevos Amigos = Phrases for New Friends 10
   ¡Cántalo! = Sing it! Alfabeto = Alphabet Song 11
   ¡Inténtalo! = Try it! A, E, I, O, U: Read Spanish In Five Minutes 12
   ¡Léelo! = Read it! Flashcards in Spanish 13
   ¡Practícalo! = Practice it! Flashcards in English 14
   ¡Juégalo! = Play it! Piñata Game 15
   ¡Míralo! = Look at it! Spanish-speakers & Hispanic-Americans 16
   ¡Hazlo! = Do it! Mi Día = My Day in Drawings 17
   ¡Cocínalo! = Cook it! Tortillas: A Soft, Round Flatbread 18
   ¡Termínalo! = Finish it! Self-Portrait Frame 19

LESSON 2: ¿CÓMO ESTÁS? = HOW ARE YOU?
   ¡Repítelo! = Repeat it! Saludos = Greetings Phrases 20
   ¡Cántalo! = Sing it! Saludos = Greetings Song 21
   ¡Inténtalo! = Try it! Pato, Pato, Ganzo = Duck, Duck, Goose Game 22
   ¡Léelo! = Read it! Flashcards in Spanish 23
   ¡Practícalo! = Practice it! Flashcards in English 24
   ¡Juégalo! = Play it! Tres En Raya = Three-In-A-Row Game 25
   ¡Míralo! = Look at it! España = Spain 26
   ¡Hazlo! = Do it! Fan & Castanets 27
   ¡Cocínalo! = Cook it! Sangría Para Niños = Sangria For Kids: A Fruity Drink 28
   ¡Termínalo! = Finish it! Las Caras = The Faces: Picasso Style 29

LESSON 3: ¿A TÍ TE GUSTA UN DEPORTE? = DO YOU LIKE A SPORT?
   ¡Repítelo! = Repeat it! Deportes = Sports Phrases 30
   ¡Cántalo! = Sing it! Deportes = Sports Song 31
   ¡Inténtalo! = Try it! Cambien = Change Places Game 32
   ¡Léelo! = Read it! Survey Book About Sports 33
   ¡Practícalo! = Practice it! Survey Book About Sports 34
   ¡Juégalo! = Play it! Touristas = Tourists: A Map Of The Spanish-Speaking Countries 35
   ¡Míralo! = Look at it! México 36
   ¡Hazlo! = Do it! Cascarones, Art For Holidays & Papel Picado 37
   ¡Cocínalo! = Cook it! Tostada: A Flat, Crisp Taco 38
   ¡Termínalo! = Finish it! Calendario Azteca = Personal Aztec Calendar 39

LESSON 4: ¿CUÁNTOS AÑOS TIENES? = HOW OLD ARE YOU?

- **¡Repítelo! = Repeat it!** Números = Numbers 1-100 Phrases 40
- **¡Cántalo! = Sing it!** Números = Numbers Song 41
- **¡Inténtalo! = Try it!** Más O Menos = More Or Less Game 42
- **¡Léelo! = Read it!** Flashcards in Spanish 43
- **¡Practícalo! = Practice it!** Flashcards in English 44
- **¡Juégalo! = Play it!** Lotería = Bingo Game 45
- **¡Míralo! = Look at it!** Central America: Guatemala, El Salvador & Honduras 46
- **¡Hazlo! = Do it!** Worry Dolls & Volcanoes 47
- **¡Cocínalo! = Cook it!** Pastel De Tres Leches = Three Milk Cake 48
- **¡Termínalo! = Finish it!** Código Maya = Mayan Code 49

LESSON 5: ¿CÓMO DICES...EN ESPAÑOL? = HOW DO YOU SAY...IN SPANISH?

- **¡Repítelo! = Repeat it!** Familia = Family Phrases 50
- **¡Cántalo! = Sing it!** Familia = Family Song 51
- **¡Inténtalo! = Try it!** Digo Un Número = I Say A Number Game 52
- **¡Léelo! = Read it!** Flashcards in Spanish 53
- **¡Practícalo! = Practice it!** Flashcards in English 54
- **¡Juégalo! = Play it!** Toma Todo = Take Everything Game 55
- **¡Míralo! = Look at it!** Central America: Nicaragua, Costa Rica & Panama 56
- **¡Hazlo! = Do it!** Name Molas & Ox Cart Wheels 57
- **¡Cocínalo! = Cook it!** Gallo Pinto: Beans & Rice Dish 58
- **¡Termínalo! = Finish it!** Proyecto De La Familia = Family Project 59

LESSON 6: ¿CUÁNDO ES TU CUMPLEAÑOS? = WHEN IS YOUR BIRTHDAY?

- **¡Repítelo! = Repeat it!** Calendario = Calendar Phrases 60
- **¡Cántalo! = Sing it!** Calendario = Calendar Song 61
- **¡Inténtalo! = Try it!** Buena Suerte = Good Luck Dice Game 62
- **¡Léelo! = Read it!** Survey About Days, Months & Birthdays 63
- **¡Practícalo! = Practice it!** Survey Book About Days, Months & Birthdays 64
- **¡Juégalo! = Play it!** Dibujos = Drawings Game 65
- **¡Míralo! = Look at it!** South America: Colombia, Venezuela & Ecuador 66
- **¡Hazlo! = Do it!** Chaquiera = Gold Jewelry & Rainsticks 67
- **¡Cocínalo! = Cook it!** Arroz Con Leche = Rice With Milk: Rice Pudding 68
- **¡Termínalo! = Finish it!** El Calendario Pequeño = Spanish Mini Calendar 69

LESSON 7: ¿QUÉ CLIMA HACE HOY? = WHAT IS THE WEATHER DOING TODAY?

- **¡Repítelo! = Repeat it!** Clima = Weather Phrases 70
- **¡Cántalo! = Sing it!** Clima = Weather Song 71
- **¡Inténtalo! = Try it!** Alrededor Del Mundo = Around The World Game 72
- **¡Léelo! = Read it!** Flashcards in Spanish 73
- **¡Practícalo! = Practice it!** Flashcards in English 74
- **¡Juégalo! = Play it!** Pares = Pairs Game 75
- **¡Míralo! = Look at it!** South America: Chile, Peru & Bolivia 76
- **¡Hazlo! = Do it!** Arpilleras = Yarn Art with Llamas & Moai Statue 77
- **¡Cocínalo! = Cook it!** Sopa de Quinua = Quinoa Soup 78
- **¡Termínalo! = Finish it!** Adivínalo = Guess It: Predict The Weather In South America 79

LESSON 8: ¿QUIERES ALGO? = DO YOU WANT SOMETHING?

- **¡Repítelo! = Repeat it!** Escuela = School Phrases 80
- **¡Cántalo! = Sing it!** Escuela = School Song 81
- **¡Inténtalo! = Try it!** La Maestra/El Maestro = The Teacher (Female/Male) game 82
- **¡Léelo! = Read it!** Flashcards in Spanish 83
- **¡Practícalo! = Practice it!** Flashcards in English 84
- **¡Juégalo! = Play it!** Mochila = Backpack game 85
- **¡Míralo! = Look at it!** South America: Argentina, Uruguay & Paraguay 86
- **¡Hazlo! = Do it!** Rastras & Boleadores de Gauchos = Cowboy Belts & Lassos 87
- **¡Cocínalo! = Cook it!** Alfajores: Cookies With Dulce De Leche 88
- **¡Termínalo! = Finish it!** El Salón Raro = The Strange Classroom 89

LESSON 9: ¿CUÁLES COLORES VES AQUÍ? = WHICH COLORES DO YOU SEE HERE?

- **¡Repítelo! = Repeat it!** Colors & Clothing Phrases 90
- **¡Cántalo! = Sing it!** Ropa De Muchos Colores = Clothing Of Many Colors Song 91
- **¡Inténtalo! = Try it!** Desfile De Moda = Fashion Show 92
- **¡Léelo! = Read it!** Survey About Colors & Clothing 93
- **¡Practícalo! = Practice it!** Survey Book About Colors & Clothing 94
- **¡Juégalo! = Play it!** Estilo De Ropa = Styles Of Clothing Game 95
- **¡Míralo! = Look at it!:** Cuba, Puerto Rico & Dominican Republic 96
- **¡Hazlo! = Do it!** Máscaras & Días Festivos = Masks & Holidays 97
- **¡Cocínalo! = Cook it!** Sándwich Cubano = Cuban Style Sandwich 98
- **¡Termínalo! = Finish it!** Mi Tienda De Ropa = My Clothing Store 99

LESSON 10: ¿QUÉ VAS A COMER? = WHAT ARE YOU GOING TO EAT?

- **¡Repítelo! = Repeat it!** Comida = Food Phrases 100
- **¡Cántalo! = Sing it!** Comida = Food Song 101
- **¡Inténtalo! = Try it!** Pásalo = Pass It Game 102
- **¡Léelo! = Read it!** Flashcards in Spanish 103
- **¡Practícalo! = Practice it!** Flashcards in English 104
- **¡Juégalo! = Play it!** Verdad O Falso = True Or False Game 105
- **¡Míralo! = Look at it!** Equatorial Guinea 106
- **¡Hazlo! = Do it!** Maracas & Cuban Piñata 107
- **¡Cocínalo! = Cook it!** Ensalada De Frutas Tropicales = Tropical Fruit Salad 108
- **¡Termínalo! = Finish it!** Un Poco Más = A Little More: Ten Ways To Practice 109
- Ten Project Ideas & Certificado = Certificate 110

APÉNDICE = APPENDIX

- Gracias From The Author Maestra Julia 111
- Supermercado = Grocery Store Scavenger Hunt 112
- Días Festivos = Holidays 114
- Examen = Exam: Questions & Answers From Each Lesson 117
- Answer Key 118
- Positive Affirmations Chart all in Spanish 120
- Classroom Commands for individuals and groups (Spanish first) 121
- Glosario = Glossary: English to Spanish 122
- Glosario = Glossary: Spanish to English 130
- Verbos y Preguntas: Verbs & Question Words 138
- Order Form 140

NOTAS = NOTES
PARA LOS ADULTOS = FOR THE ADULTS:

1. **10 lecciones = 10 lessons:** Each of the 10 lessons will take about two hours to complete. You may divide them and work on a few pages each time. There is one conversational question and answer along with 10 phrases.

2. **Tú vs. Usted = 2 Ways of Saying "You":** This book is written in the "Tú" form for elementary students to talk with each other and their families. Look ahead at pp.114-116 for **Días festivos = Holiday** activities. For adults to learn Spanish with the "Usted" form try our *Spanish Chatbook* series of conversational workbooks found at SpanishChatCompany.com.

3. **Para toda la Familia = For the Whole Family:** This book is for classes and families to enjoy together.

4. **Introducción = Introduction:** The first time a phrase or word is introduced, it will have the Spanish phrase followed by the English phrase and finally the pronunciation guide in italics. This guide is meant to help a native English speaker read the Spanish phrase out loud and pronounce the words correctly.

5. **Pronunciación = Pronunciation:** Each new word in the pronunciation guide is capitalized. For example, nice to meet you = mucho gusto *(Moo-cho Goose-toh)*. Two vowels are sometimes combined as indicated by a slash: Well = Bien *(Bee/ehn)*. A word with an accent mark means that the syllable is stressed and should be emphasized when spoken. For example, in the phrase "How are you? = ¿Cómo estás? *(KOH-moh Ehs-TAHS?)*," the accent mark indicates putting the emphasis on the "KOH" and the "TAHS."

6. **Spanglish = Spanish + English:** Many native speakers say the same sentence in a variety of ways. "How are you?," "How are you doing?," "How is it going?" & "What's up?" These all ask the same question. None of the ways are wrong. They are just different styles. In this *Elementary Spanish Chatbook*, I have chosen one way of saying a phrase or a vocabulary word and you will review that same phrase over and over. This is less confusing for elementary-school children. I've tried to use correct phrases without being too formal.

7. **¡Inténtalo! = Try it!:** In each lesson, there is a group game. If you are working through this book individually, you may want to find friends or family to assist. You may need to adapt difficult activities for your child.

8. **Buena suerte y una sonrisa de parte de tu Maestra Julia. = Good luck and a smile from your teacher Julie:** I love your feedback, and I encourage you to please contact me with any suggestions and comments. Find more information at SpanishChatCompany.com

GROUP COMMANDS

Give these commands to the whole class and use them in "The Teacher Says" game on page 82. For individual commands in Spanish first see page 121.

Add up = **Sumen**	Open = **Abren**
Answer = **Contesten**	Pass = **Pasen**
Ask = **Pregunten**	Pick up = **Recojan**
Bring = **Traigan**	Play = **Jueguen**
Choose = **Escojan**	Point to = **Señalen**
Close = **Cierren**	Practice = **Practiquen**
Color = **Coloreen**	Put = **Pongan**
Come = **Vengan**	Read = **Lean**
Cook = **Cocinen**	Repeat = **Repitan**
Count = **Cuenten**	Respond = **Respondan**
Cut = **Corten**	Say = **Digan**
Cut out = **Recorten**	Show = **Muestren**
Draw = **Dibujen**	Sing = **Canten**
End = **Terminen**	Sit down = **Siéntense**
Enter = **Entren**	Stand up = **Levántense**
Erase = **Borren**	Stop = **Párense**
Finish = **Terminen**	Take = **Tomen**
Fold = **Doblen**	Take off = **Quiten**
Follow = **Sigan**	Take out = **Saquen**
Give = **Den**	Talk = **Hablen**
Go = **Vayan**	Throw = **Tiren**
Hop = **Den un saltito**	Touch = **Toquen**
Jump = **Salten**	Try = **Intenten**
Leave = **Salgan**	Turn = **Giran / Doblen**
Listen = **Escuchen**	Turn around = **Dense una vuelta**
Look = **Miren**	Walk = **Anden**
Look for = **Busquen**	Write = **Escriban**

ELEMENTARY SPANISH CHATBOOK © SPANISH CHAT COMPANY

MOVIES & AUDIO

Would you like to hear the songs and sing along?
Wish you could practice in the car or at home?
Want to hear these Spanish words pronounced correctly?

Our *Elementary Spanish Chatbook* Audio Tracks (CD's) and *Spanish Chatshow* Movies (DVD's) are now available. Enjoy listening to over 100 conversational vocabulary words and phases while watching the sign language or viewing the Kids' cooking shows. Sing-along during the 10 songs designed specifically for kids. Purchase the Audio Tracks and *Spanish Chatshow* movies now to improve pronunciation and learn Spanish through fun songs and activities. Each time you see the above symbols in the book, you will be able to watch a movie or sing to improve your Spanish skills. Pair the book and audio together with our *Spanish Chatshow* movies to maximize your learning experience! Order everything now from SpanishChatCompany.com.

ELEMENTARY SPANISH CHATBOOK AUDIO TRACKS

1. Lesson 1 *p. 11* **Alfabeto = Alphabet song** to the melody of "La Raspa"
2. Lesson 2 *p. 21* **Saludos = Greetings song** to the melody of "Skip to my Lou"
3. Lesson 3 *p. 31* **Deportes = Sports song** to the melody of "London Bridge"
4. Lesson 4 *p. 41* **Números = Numbers song** to the melody of "Farmer in the Dell"
5. Lesson 5 *p. 51* **Familia = Family song** to the melody of "Un Elefante"
6. Lesson 6 *p. 61* **Calendario = Calendar song** to the melody of "Mary Had a Little Lamb"
7. Lesson 7 *p. 71* **Clima = Weather song** to the melody of "La Cucaracha"
8. Lesson 8 *p. 81* **Escuela = School song** to the melody of "Cielito Lindo"
9. Lesson 9 *p. 91* **Ropa de Muchos Colores = Clothing of Many Colors song** to the melody of "Row, Row, Row Your Boat"
10. Lesson 10 *p. 101* **Comida = Food song** to the melody of "Los Pollitos"
11. **Final Credits & Gracias from Maestra Julia**
12. **Final Track-** *from p. 21* **See you Later** the last verse of the "Saludos = Greetings Song."

SPANISH CHATSHOW MOVIES

¡REPÍTELO! = REPEAT IT!

Sign language, English and Spanish vocabulary

1. Lesson 1 *pp. 10 & 11* **Nuevos Amigos = New Friends**
2. Lesson 2 *pp. 20 & 21* **Saludos = Greetings**
3. Lesson 3 *pp. 30 & 31* **Deportes = Sports**
4. Lesson 4 *pp. 40 & 41* **Números = Numbers**
5. Lesson 5 *pp. 50 & 51* **Familia = Family**
6. Lesson 6 *pp. 60 & 61* **Calendario = Calendar**
7. Lesson 7 *pp. 70 & 71* **Clima = Weather**
8. Lesson 8 *pp. 80 & 81* **Escuela = School**
9. Lesson 9 *pp. 90 & 91* **Colores y Ropa = Colores & Clothing**
10. Lesson 10 *pp. 100 & 101* **Comida = Food**

¡CÁNTALO! = SING IT!

Spanish Music Videos / English Music Videos

11. Lesson 1 *p. 13* **Alphabet**
12. Lesson 2 *p. 23* **Greetings**
13. Lesson 3 *p. 33* **Sports**
14. Lesson 4 *p. 43* **Numbers**
15. Lesson 5 *p. 53* **Family**
16. Lesson 6 *p. 63* **Calendar**
17. Lesson 7 *p. 73* **Weather**
18. Lesson 8 *p. 83* **School**
19. Lesson 9 *p. 93* **Clothing of Many Colors**
20. Lesson 10 *p. 103* **Food**

ELEMENTARY SPANISH CHATBOOK

LECCIÓN = LESSON	VERBO = VERB	TEMA = SUBJECT	CULTURA = CULTURE
1	llamar = to be called	New Friends & Alphabet	Hispanics in the U.S.A.
2	estar = to be	Greetings	Spain
3	gustar = to like	Sports	Mexico
4	tener = to have	Numbers 1-100	Guatemala, El Salvador, Honduras
5	decir = to say	Family	Nicaragua, Costa Rica, Panama
6	ser = to be	Months & Weekdays	Colombia, Venezuela, Ecuador
7	hacer = to do / to make	Weather	Chile, Peru, Bolivia
8	querer = to want	School	Argentina, Uruguay, Paraguay
9	ver = to see	Clothing & Colors	Dominican Republic, Cuba, Puerto Rico
10	ir a /comer = to go / to eat	Food	Equatorial Guinea

NOMBRES = NAMES

Use the "Name" list to choose a Spanish name and write it on the line below. Some English names do not translate into Spanish, so use your middle name or choose a name that starts with the same letter as your name.

Me llamo _____. = My name is...
(Meh Yah-moh...)

Add your Spanish and English names to the nametag on the next page and decorate it using lots of bright colors. In Latin America, you would use two last names—your mother's maiden name and your father's name.

NIÑAS = GIRLS

Adriana	Carolina	Gabriela	Lupe	Paula
Alejandra	Carlota	Gloria	Margarita	Rebeca
Alicia	Cecilia	Graciela	María	Raquel
Alma	Clara	Hilda	Maribel	Rosa
Amalia	Cristina	Inés	Maricarmen	Sandra
Ana	Diana	Isabel	Maricela	Sara
Andrea	Dora	Juana	Marisol	Sofía
Ángela	Elena	Julia	Marta	Susana
Beatriz	Esmeralda	Laura	Mercedes	Teresa
Blanca	Ester	Liliana	Mónica	Victoria
Carmen	Eva	Linda	Olga	Yolanda

NIÑOS = BOYS

Adán	Daniel	Gerardo	Juan	Pedro
Alberto	David	Gonzalo	Julio	Rafael
Alejandro	Diego	Gregorio	Luis	Ramón
Alfonso	Eduardo	Guillermo	Manuel	Raúl
Alfredo	Emilio	Héctor	Marcos	Roberto
Andrés	Enrique	Jaime	Mario	Rubén
Antonio	Ernesto	Javier	Mateo	Samuel
Arturo	Felipe	Jesús	Miguel	Santiago
Bernardo	Félix	Joaquín	Nicolás	Timoteo
Carlos	Fernando	Jorge	Oscar	Tomás
César	Francisco	José	Pablo	Victor

9 NUEVE

Recorta = Cut out along the dashed lines

En español me llamo _____
(Spanish name)

My English name is _____

Learn Spanish Today for Work & Play

SPANISH CHAT COMPANY

LECCIÓN  LESSON

LLAMAR(SE) = TO BE NAMED (CALLED)

¿CÓMO TE LLAMAS? = WHAT IS YOUR NAME?

- 🌎 Learn How To Read & Chat In Spanish In Five Minutes
- 🌎 Nuevos Amigos = Phrases For Your New Friends
- 🌎 Alfabeto = Alphabet
- 🌎 Spanish-Speakers & Hispanic-Americans
- 🌎 Arte = Art: Illustrate Your Day
- 🌎 Comida = Food: Tortillas, Pupusas & Arepas
- 🌎 Tarea = Homework: Frame

LECCIÓN 1

 ¡REPÍTELO! = REPEAT IT!

Draw a picture to illustrate each word or phrase. Repeat these to your **nuevos amigos = new friends**.

Buenos días. *(Bweh-nohs DEE-ahs.)* Good morning. / Good day.	**Buenas tardes.** *(Bweh-nahs Tahr-dehs.)* Good afternoon. / Good evening. (12 p.m. – dark)	**Buenas noches.** *(Bweh-nahs Noh-chehs.)* Good night.
Hola. *(Oh-lah.)* Hello.	**¿Cómo te llamas?** *(KOH-moh Teh Yah-mahs?)* What is your name?	**Me llamo _____.** *(Meh Yah-moh...)* My name is...
Mucho gusto. *(Moo-cho Goose-toh.)* Nice to meet you. / Much pleasure.	**Hasta luego.** *(Ahs-tah Loo/eh-goh.)* See you later. / Until later.	**¡Adiós amigos!** *(Ah-dee/OHS! Ah-mee-gohs!)* Goodbye friends!

ELEMENTARY SPANISH CHATBOOK ©SPANISH CHAT COMPANY

LECCIÓN 1

11 ONCE

♪¡CÁNTALO! = SING IT!

Listen and sing the Spanish alphabet song. There are 27 letters with the extra letter ñ. The letters, rr, ch and ll are no longer considered distinct letters. While you are singing, do the Raspa dance with a partner. Start with left heel, right heel, left heel clap clap. Now right heel first and repeat this part four times. During the faster alphabet part, link elbows with your partner and twirl. This song also can be used to select a student to be a helper or point out each person who is sitting quietly.

ALFABETO = ALPHABET
Melody: Jarabe Tapatío = Mexican Hat dance   Key of F

A	ah		J	hoh-tah		R	ehr-reh
B	beh		K	kah		S	ehs-seh
C	seh		L	ehl-leh		T	teh
D	deh		M	ehm-meh		U	oo
E	eh		N	ehn-neh		V	oo-veh
F	ehf-feh		Ñ	ehn-ñyeh		W	doh-bleh-veh
G	heh		O	oh		X	eh-kees
H	ah-cheh		P	peh		Y	ee-gree-eh-gah
I	eee		Q	koo		Z	seh-tah

ELEMENTARY SPANISH CHATBOOK ©SPANISH CHAT COMPANY

LECCIÓN 1

12 DOCE

¡INTÉNTALO! = TRY IT!

A, E, I, O, U

LEARN TO READ SPANISH IN FIVE MINUTES

The good news is, the vowels are always the same!

A (AH)	banana *(Bah-nah-nah)* = banana mamá y papá *(Mah-MAH y Pah-PAH)* = mom and dad
E (EH)	maestra / maestro *(Ma/ehs-trah/troh)* = teacher (female/male) bebé *(Beh-BEH)* = baby
I (EEE)	sí *(See)* = yes qui-qui-ri-quí *(Kee-kee-ree-KEE)* = cock-a-doodle-doo
O (OH)	no *(Noh)* = no ¿Cómo? *(KOH-moh?)* = How's that?
U (OO) as in moon	Mucho gusto. *(Moo-cho Goose-toh.)* = Nice to meet you.

LA MARACA

A game similar to "Hot Potato"

To play "La Maraca" = "The Maraca," first form a circle. Now sing along with the song below, and fill in the blanks for three students each time. Use rainsticks, maracas, drums, or some other instrument to provide rhythm. Then play "hot potato" with a maraca. Pass one maraca around the circle and stop at the end of the song. The person left holding the maraca has to go introduce himself or herself in Spanish to someone else. The full song can be found on page 21 = veintiuno. The melody is "Skip to My Lou."

A, E, I, O, U,
¿Cómo te llamas tú?
A, E, I, O, U,
¿Cómo te llamas tú?

Me llamo _____. ¿Y tú?
Me llamo _____. ¿Y tú?
Me llamo _____. ¿Y tú?
Mucho gusto. Mucho gusto.

ELEMENTARY SPANISH CHATBOOK   ©SPANISH CHAT COMPANY

 **¡LÉELO!** = READ IT!

LECCIÓN 1

13 TRECE

Decorate an envelope to hold these flashcards.
Cut them out and play "La Piñata" game from p. 15 = quince.   Recorta = Cut out along the dashed lines

Buenos días.
(Bweh-nohs Dee-ahs.)

LECCIÓN 1

Buenas tardes.
(Bweh-nahs Tahr-dehs.)

LECCIÓN 1

Buenas noches.
(Bweh-nahs Noh-chehs.)

LECCIÓN 1

Hola.
(Oh-lah.)

LECCIÓN 1

¿Cómo te llamas?
(KOH-moh Teh Yah-mahs?)

LECCIÓN 1

Me llamo _____.
(Meh Yah-moh...)

LECCIÓN 1

Mucho gusto.
(Moo-cho Goose-toh.)

LECCIÓN 1

Hasta luego.
(Ahs-tah Loo/eh-goh.)

LECCIÓN 1

¡Adiós amigos!
(Ah-dee/OHS! Ah-mee-gohs!)

LECCIÓN 1

ELEMENTARY SPANISH CHATBOOK   ©SPANISH CHAT COMPANY

LECCIÓN 1

¡PRACTÍCALO! = PRACTICE IT!

Play the "La Piñata" game from p. 15 = quince using these flashcards.

Recorta = Cut out along the dashed lines

Good night.

Good afternoon.
Good evening.
(12 p.m. – dark)

Good morning. /
Good day.

My name is...

What is your name?

Hello.

Goodbye friends!

See you later.

Nice to meet you.

ELEMENTARY SPANISH CHATBOOK   ©SPANISH CHAT COMPANY

LECCIÓN 1

¡JUÉGALO! = PLAY IT!

15 QUINCE

LA PIÑATA
A game similar to "Hangman"

PERDÓN = SORRY

1. To play "La Piñata" = "The Piñata," choose one Spanish word from any flashcard. Or, to make it more difficult, use a Spanish word or phrase from the glosario = glossary pages 122-137, a Spanish number from page 40 or the name of a classmate. To pronounce the alphabet in Spanish go back to page 11.

2. Write down the exact number of lines to correspond to each letter in the word. For example, Student #1 would write ___ ___ ___ ___ for four letters in the word "Hola."

3. Student #2 guesses a letter such as B. "Perdón, no hay la letra B. = Sorry, but there is no B." Then Student #2 fills in a triangle on the piñata.

4. Student #1 now guesses any letter to try to solve Student #2's word.

5. The first person to guess the correct word wins. If you fill your piñata, you lose the game.

Latin Americans have been using candies and small toys to fill up piñatas for many years. A star-shaped piñata represents the Star of Bethlehem during Las Posadas. There are many different styles of piñatas In Cuba, they attach strings to the piñata and instead of using a bat, everyone grabs a string and pulls the piñata apart. Buy a piñata or make your own for your next celebration.

ELEMENTARY SPANISH CHATBOOK ©SPANISH CHAT COMPANY

LECCIÓN 1

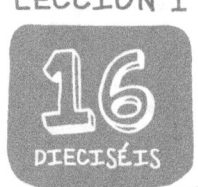 **¡MÍRALO!** = LOOK AT IT!

Latina? Hispanic? Chicano? Mexican? Which one is the correct term to use? To find out, read this sunflower = girasol. This flower turns = girar to the sun = sol. During Hispanic Heritage Month—September 15–October 15—check for local events celebrating Hispanic culture and achievements of Hispanic Americans. For more about fiestas in Latin America see holiday pages 114-116 = ciento catorce hasta ciento dieciséis.

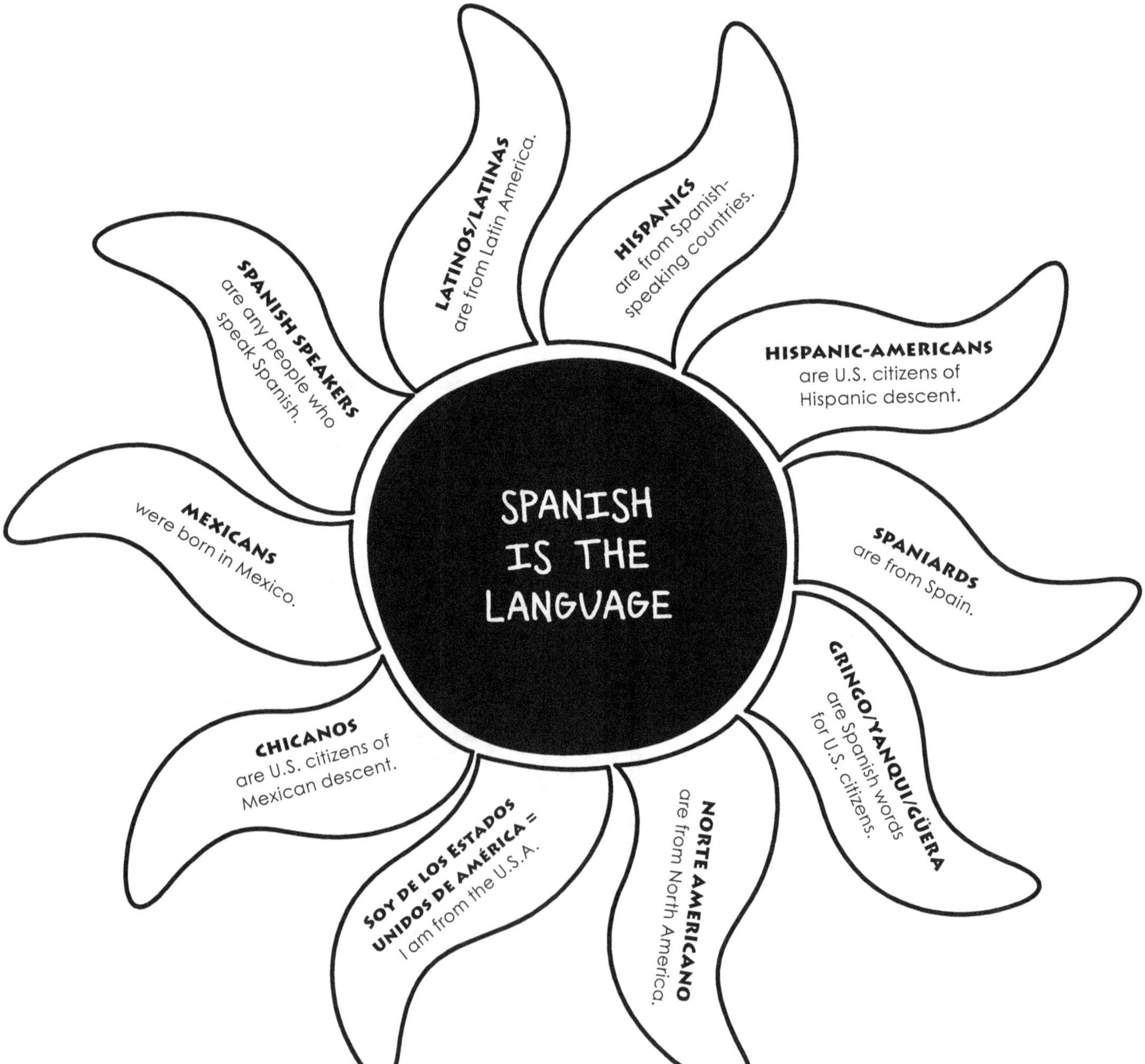

SPANISH IS THE LANGUAGE

- **LATINOS/LATINAS** are from Latin America.
- **HISPANICS** are from Spanish-speaking countries.
- **SPANISH SPEAKERS** are any people who speak Spanish.
- **HISPANIC-AMERICANS** are U.S. citizens of Hispanic descent.
- **MEXICANS** were born in Mexico.
- **SPANIARDS** are from Spain.
- **CHICANOS** are U.S. citizens of Mexican descent.
- **GRINGO/YANQUI/GÜERA** are Spanish words for U.S. citizens.
- **SOY DE LOS ESTADOS UNIDOS DE AMÉRICA** = I am from the U.S.A.
- **NORTE AMERICANO** are from North America.

 **¡HAZLO!** = DO IT!

LECCIÓN 1

17 DIECISIETE

MI DÍA = MY DAY

Draw a picture of what you do during each part of your day. You may also make a poster or a cartoon. Look around your house and find something written in Spanish or an item made in Latin America. Bring it next time for Show and Tell.

BUENOS DÍAS

BUENAS TARDES

BUENAS NOCHES

LECCIÓN 1

18 DIECIOCHO ¡COCÍNALO! = COOK IT!

Try making the following recipe. It is popular throughout Latin America:

TORTILLAS, AREPAS, PUPUSAS, GORDITAS, QUESADILLAS

Remember that an adult will need to help you with anything hot.

TORTILLAS / AREPAS / PUPUSAS / GORDITAS / QUESADILLAS

1. <u>Primero haga la masa.</u> = First make the dough. Empieza con la harina preparada para tortillas. = Start with the flour that is prepared for tortillas. Hay maíz blanco, maíz amarillo, maíz azul, trigo o harina de arroz. = There is either white corn, yellow corn, blue corn, wheat, or rice flour.

2. <u>Añade sal y agua tibia.</u> = Add salt and warm water according to the package.

3. <u>Mezcla la masa.</u> = Mix the dough and let it rest for about 15 minutes.

4. <u>Haga una bola.</u> = Make a ball with the dough.

5. <u>Oprima la bola.</u> = Press the dough flat with a tortilla press. If you don't have a tortilla press, push a plate down onto the dough to cut a circle or press the tortilla into a circle with your hands. You may want to use wax paper on each side of the dough ball to prevent it from sticking to the tortilla press. To make arepas, pupusas or gorditas, follow the same steps, but make the dough thicker.

6. <u>Cocina la tortilla.</u> = Cook the tortilla. Have an adult help you cook it for just a few minutes on each side using an electric skillet, griddle or sauté pan.

7. <u>Pon la mantequilla encima de la tortilla.</u> Put the butter on top of the tortilla.

8. <u>Añade la canela y azúcar.</u> = Add the cinnamon and sugar. Opcional: Añade frijoles, carne molida, carne asada, pollo, camarones, queso, salsa o aguacate. = Optional: Add beans, hamburger, grilled meat, chicken, shrimp, cheese, sauce or avocado.

9. <u>¡Cómela!</u> = Eat it! ¡Mmmm, qué rico! = How tasty!

10. <u>¡Buen provecho!</u> = Bon appetit! Disfruta tus tortillas = Enjoy your tortillas.

TORTILLAS: These are made from corn or wheat flour. Torta means cake in Spain, and tortillas means little cakes.

QUESADILLAS: Corn or wheat flour tortillas with cheese inside. Other ingredients such as squash blossoms or meat can be included.

AREPAS: These are thicker corn tortillas found in South America, sometimes filled with cheese, beans or meat.

PUPUSAS AND GORDITAS: These are thicker than tortillas, made out of corn or rice flour and they are stuffed with cheese, beans or pork.

🏠 **¡TERMÍNALO!** = FINISH IT!

LECCIÓN 1

19
DIECINUEVE

Color the picture frame below. Cut out the center of the rectangle and put in a picture of yourself and your friends dressed in Latin attire or with a giant sombrero. Attach a magnet on the back and hang it on your refrigerator or glue it to the inside front cover of this book. Try to use the positive Spanish phrases every day. A list of affirmations is on page 120 = ciento veinte.

- maravilloso
- fantástico
- perfecto
- correcto
- mi favorito
- super
- excelente
- fabuloso

ELEMENTARY SPANISH CHATBOOK © SPANISH CHAT COMPANY

LECCIÓN  LESSON

ESTAR = TO BE

¿CÓMO ESTÁS? = HOW ARE YOU?

- 🌎 Saludos = Greetings
- 🌎 España = Spain
- 🌎 Arte = Art: Abanicos & Castañuelas
- 🌎 Comida = Food: Sangria For Kids
- 🌎 Tarea = Homework: Pablo Picasso Faces

LECCIÓN 2

 ¡REPÍTELO! = REPEAT IT!

Draw a picture to illustrate each word or phrase. Repeat them in Spanish. ¡Increíble! = Incredible!

¿Cómo estás? (KOH-moh Ehs-TAHS?) How are you?	**Estoy bien.** (Ehs-toh/ee Bee/ehn.) I am well.	**Estoy muy mal.** (Ehs-toh/ee Moo/ee Mahl.) I am very bad.
Estoy enferma / enfermo . (Ehs-toh/ee Ehn-fehr-mah / Ehn-fehr-moh.) I am sick (girl / boy).	**Estoy cansada / cansado.** (Ehs-toh/ee Kahn-sah-dah / Kahn-sah-doh.) I am tired. (girl / boy)	**¡Pobrecita!** (Poh-breh-see-tah) Oh you poor girl!
¡Pobrecito! (Poh-breh-see-toh!) Oh you poor boy!	**Estoy muy feliz.** (Ehs-toh/ee Moo/ee Feh-leez.) I am very happy.	**¿Y tú?** (Ee TOO?) And you?

ELEMENTARY SPANISH CHATBOOK ©Spanish Chat Company

Listen and sing along with this song using maracas or other instruments. Act out the song using exaggerated signs. You may want to turn off the lights, "Apaguen las luces," during the "Buenas noches" verse. Turn them back on "Encienden las luces" for the next verse. Sing parts of this song during the beginning and ending of each lesson.

SALUDOS = GREETINGS
Melody: Skip To My Lou   Key of D

Buenos días. ¿Cómo estás?
Buenos días. ¿Cómo estás?
Buenos días. ¿Cómo estás?
¿Cómo estás tú?

Estoy bien. ¿Y tú?
Estoy bien. ¿Y tú?
Estoy bien. ¿Y tú?
Estoy muy feliz.

Buenas tardes. ¿Cómo estás?
Buenas tardes. ¿Cómo estás?
Buenas tardes. ¿Cómo estás?
¿Cómo estás tú?

Estoy enferma. ¿Y tú?
Estoy enfermo. ¿Y tú?
Estoy enferma. ¿Y tú?
Estoy muy mal.

Buenas noches. ¿Cómo estás?
Buenas noches. ¿Cómo estás?
Buenas noches. ¿Cómo estás?
¿Cómo estás tú?

Estoy cansado. ¿Y tú?
Estoy cansada. ¿Y tú?
Estoy cansado. ¿Y tú?
¡Pobrecita y pobrecito!

A, E, I, O, U,
¿Cómo te llamas tú?
A, E, I, O, U,
¿Cómo te llamas tú?

Me llamo Maestra. ¿Y tú?
Me llamo Maestro. ¿Y tú?
Me llamo _____. ¿Y tú?
Mucho gusto. Mucho gusto.

Hasta luego. ¡Cha-cha-cha!
Hasta luego. ¡Cha-cha-cha!
¡Adiós amigos!
¡Adiós amigos!

LECCIÓN 2

¡INTÉNTALO! = TRY IT!

PATO, PATO, GANZO
A game similar to "Duck, Duck, Goose"

CABEZAS = HEADS

1. To play "Pato, Pato, Ganzo" = "Duck, Duck, Goose," choose one person to be the "granjera" = "female farmer." (granjero = male farmer)

2. "Granjera" goes around the círculo = circle lightly touching cabezas = heads with one finger and saying, "pato, pato…" = "duck, duck…."

3. "Granjera" taps one person's head and, instead of saying "pato," they will say, "ganso." = goose.

4. Both children run in opposite directions around the circle.

5. When they meet each other halfway, they shake hands and introduce themselves.

6. "Granjera" says, "¿Cómo te llamas?" Ganso replies, "Me llamo _____. ¿Cómo te llamas?" "Granjera" says, "Me llamo _____. Mucho gusto." Ganso says, "mucho gusto."

7. You may also say, "Cómo estás?" and answer with any of the phrases from this lesson.

8. Now they both run in opposite directions to try to be the first person to sit in the open spot. The person that is left out then becomes the "granjera/granjero."

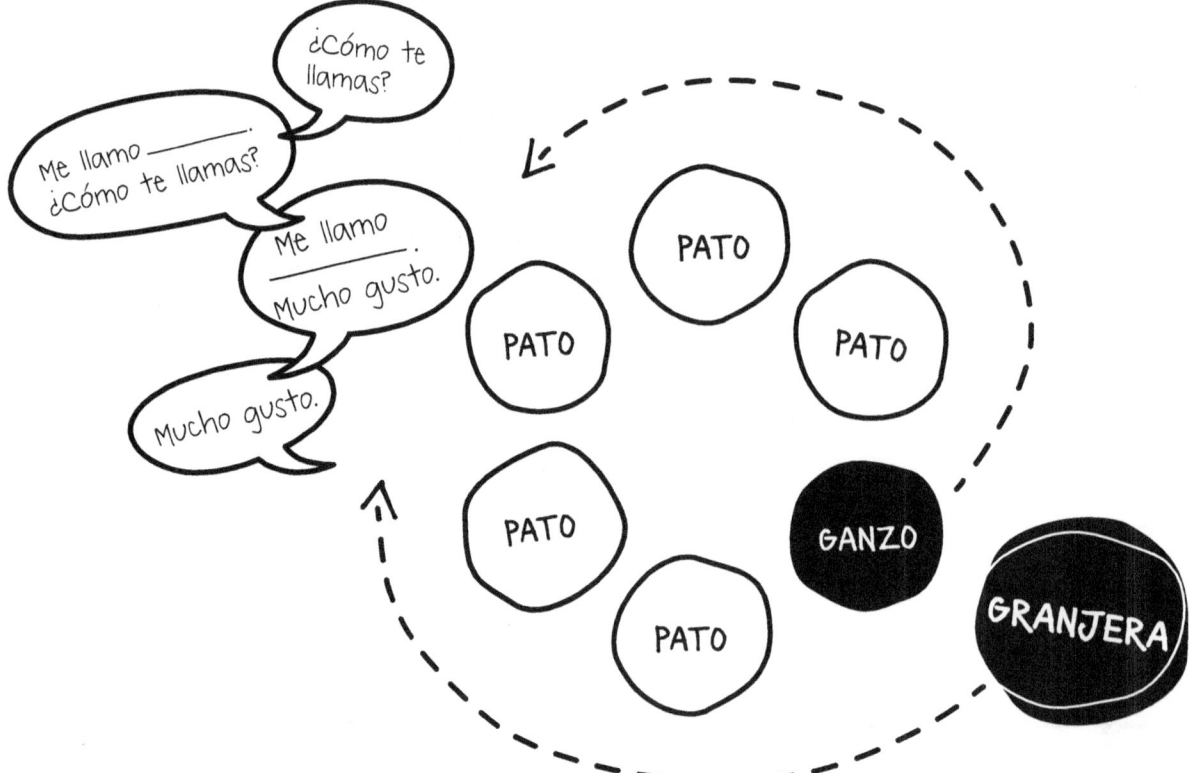

ELEMENTARY SPANISH CHATBOOK   ©SPANISH CHAT COMPANY

 **¡LÉELO!** = READ IT!

LECCIÓN 2

23
VEINTITRÉS

Cut these flashcards out and play the "Tres en Raya" game from p. 25 = veinticinco or play charades.

Recorta = Cut out along the dashed lines

¿Cómo estás?
(KOH-moh Ehs-TAHS?)

LECCIÓN 2

Estoy bien.
(Ehs-toh/ee Bee/ehn.)

LECCIÓN 2

Estoy muy mal.
(Ehs-toh/ee Moo/ee Mahl.)

LECCIÓN 2

Estoy enferma / enfermo.
*(Ehs-toh/ee Ehn-fehr-mah
Oh Ehn-fehr-moh.)*

LECCIÓN 2

¡Pobrecito!
(Poh-breh-see-toh!)

LECCIÓN 2

¡Pobrecita!
(Poh-breh-see-tah)

LECCIÓN 2

¿Y tú?
(Ee TOO?)

LECCIÓN 2

Estoy muy feliz.
(Ehs-toh/ee Moo/ee Feh-leez.)

LECCIÓN 2

Estoy cansada / cansado.
*(Ehs-toh/ee Kahn-sah-dah
Oh Kahn-sah-doh.)*

LECCIÓN 2

ELEMENTARY SPANISH CHATBOOK

©SPANISH CHAT COMPANY

LECCIÓN 2

¡PRACTÍCALO! = PRACTICE IT!

Cut these flashcards out and use them to play the "Tres en Raya" game on p. 25 = veinticinco.

Recorta = Cut out along the dashed lines

I am very bad.

I am well.

How are you?

Oh you poor girl!

Oh you poor boy!

I am a sick.
(girl / boy)

I am tired.
(girl / boy)

I am very happy.

And you?

ELEMENTARY SPANISH CHATBOOK ©SPANISH CHAT COMPANY

TRES EN RAYA
A game similar to "Tic-tac-toe"

 ¡JUÉGALO! = PLAY IT!

LECCIÓN 2

To play "Tres en Raya" = "Three in a Row," use any nine flashcards. Student #1 removes one of the flashcards, says the phrase in Spanish and places an X in that square. Next, Student #2 removes any flashcard from this same board, says it in Spanish and places the O on that space. Try to get three in a line to win.

LECCIÓN 2

 ¡MÍRALO! = LOOK AT IT!

ESPAÑA = SPAIN

CIUDAD CAPITAL = CAPITAL CITY

MADRID

DINERO = MONEY

EURO

BANDERA = FLAG

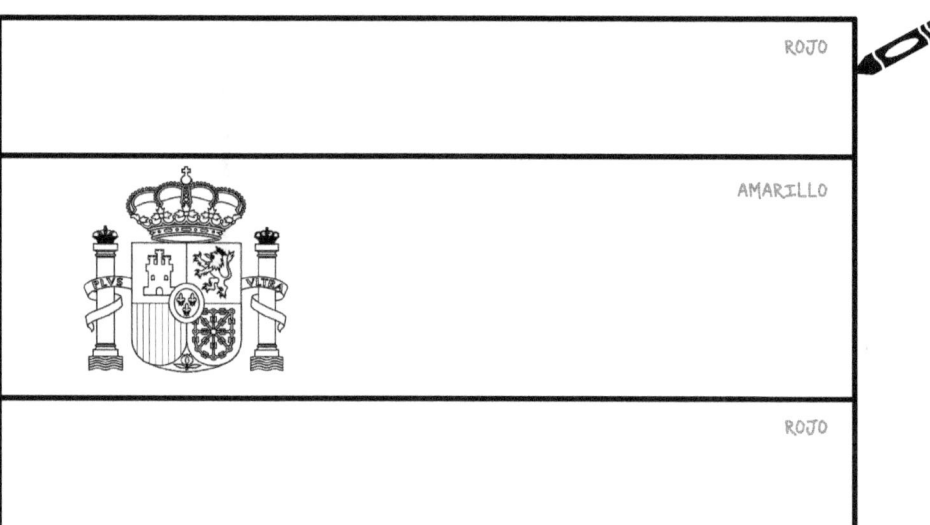

ROJO

AMARILLO

ROJO

WHICH ONE IS FALSE? (2 ARE TRUE, SO PUT AN X BY THE FALSE ONE)

Take a class vote. Ask each person to guess if #1, 2 or 3 is the false answer by holding up 1, 2 or 3 fingers. The answers are on p. 118 = ciento dieciocho in the back of this book.

1. The building of the Antoni Gaudí Sagrada familia church in Barcelona is expected to be complete in 2026.

2. A tapa/appetizer named "Calamares en su Tinta" = Squid in its own ink can turn your mouth black as you eat it.

3. If you order a "Tortilla con Queso" in Spain, you would get something like a quesadilla with a soft flour taco shell.

LECCIÓN 2

¡HAZLO! = DO IT!

27
VEINTISIETE

ABANICO = FAN

Fans are used in Spain to cool down during the hot afternoons. Waving the fan can have different meanings. If you wave it quickly, it can mean "I like you." Waving it slowly means "I'm not interested."

1. Open a coffee filter or a paper towel.
2. Use washable markers or water color paints to add designs.
3. Add Spanish words or phrases with a permanent marker or colored pencil.
4. Then spray with water and let dry overnight.
5. Alternate folding it back and forth.
6. Secure it with a pipe cleaner or colored popsicle stick handle.

CASTAÑUELAS = CASTANETS

Castaña = chestnut is the wood usually used to make these hand percussion instruments. Castanets are used during "Sevillana" folk dancing and some styles of Flamenco.

1. Cut a paper plate in half and then fold each half to make two rounded triangle castanets.
2. Students can decorate with markers or paint.
3. ADULT: Super Glue two washers, pennies or flattened bottle caps on one inside edge and two on the other inside edge so they will clink together when you use it.
4. Punch two holes in each side about a half inch apart. Put a rubber band through the holes on one side and tie it on the inside so the outside will have a loop for your fingers to go through.
5. Practice the Flamenco dance. ¡Ole!

FLAMENCO = FLAMINGO

Learn the four basic arm movements below for the flamenco dance. Use your castanets to practice as you listen to Flamenco music.

Coje la manzana. = Pick the apple.
Come la manzana. = Eat the apple.
Tira la manzana. = Throw the apple.
Pisa la manzana. = Stomp the apple.

ELEMENTARY SPANISH CHATBOOK   ©SPANISH CHAT COMPANY

LECCIÓN 2

 ¡COCÍNALO! = COOK IT!

Try making the following recipe from Spain:

SANGRÍA PARA NIÑOS = SANGRIA FOR KIDS

You may want to find the recipe for "Tortilla de patata" and make the egg/potato omelet or any other "tapas"= appetizers to go with your sangria. Tapas originated because restaurant owners put a plate on top of each drink to keep the flies away, then they added a little sample of food on those plates.

SANGRÍA PARA NIÑOS

1. Haz el jugo en una jarra grande. = Make the juice in a large pitcher.
2. Añade 2 tazas de jugo de uva. = Add 2 cups of grape juice.
3. Añade 1 taza de jugo de arándano. = Add 1 cup of cranberry juice.
4. Añade 1 taza de jugo de naranja. = Add 1 cup of orange juice. You may use other juice combinations.
5. Exprime el jugo de un limón. = Squeeze the juice of 1 lemon.
6. Añade 3 tazas de refresco. = Add 3 cups of lemon-lime carbonated soft drink.
7. Mezcla los jugos. = Mix the juices. Add more grape juice to make it taste sweeter.
8. Corta las manzanas, peras y naranjas y ponlas en la jarra. = Cut up apples, pears and oranges and put them in the pitcher.
9. ¡Bébelo! = Drink it.
10. ¡Mmmm, qué rico! = How tasty! ¡Buen provecho! = Bon appetit! Disfruta tu bebida de sangría. = Enjoy your sangria drink.

PANAMÁ: Using fruit from the rainforest, make a papaya, pineapple, peach, coconut or mango smoothie.

COSTA RICA: Fresco de frutas in Costa Rica is made by placing tropical fruits in a glass and then pouring a strawberry syrup over the top.

AGUAS FRESCAS: A drink that is sold on the streets of Mexico, Central America and the Caribbean. Fruits of many flavors, seeds flowers and even cereals are mixed with water to make this refreshing drink that is often sold by the glass.

LECCIÓN 2

 ¡TERMÍNALO! = FINISH IT!

29
VEINTINUEVE

LAS CARAS = THE FACES

Make a Pablo Picasso face for each emotion. Draw the ojos = eyes, boca = mouth, dientes = teeth, nariz = nose, pelo = hair and orejas = ears all mixed up in Picasso style. For example, one of the eyes could be in the mouth position. It is also fun to cut face parts from magazines and glue them randomly onto these six boxes. Share your work with the class at the beginning of the next lesson. Use the back of this paper if you need extra space.

Estoy bien.	Estoy cansada o cansado.	Estoy enferma o enfermo.
Estoy triste.	Estoy muy feliz.	Estoy muy mal.

ELEMENTARY SPANISH CHATBOOK ©SPANISH CHAT COMPANY

LECCIÓN 3 LESSON

GUSTAR = TO LIKE

¿A TÍ TE GUSTA UN DEPORTE? = DO YOU LIKE A SPORT?

- 🌎 Deportes = Sports
- 🌎 México
- 🌎 Mapa = Map Of The Spanish-speaking Countries
- 🌎 Arte = Art: Cascarones & Papel picado
- 🌎 Comida = Food: Tostadas
- 🌎 Tarea = Homework: Calendario Azteca

LECCIÓN 3

 ¡REPÍTELO! = REPEAT IT!

Draw a picture to illustrate each word or phrase. Repeat them in Spanish. ¡Magnífico! = Magnificent!

¿A tí te gusta un deporte? *(Ah TEE, Teh Goose-tah Oon Deh-pohr-teh?)* Do you like a sport?	**A mí me gusta el fútbol.** *(Ah MEE Meh Goose-tah Ehl FOOOOT-bohl.)* I like soccer.	**¿Preparados? ¿Listos? ¡Ya!** *(Preh-pah-rah-dohs? Lees-tohs? Yah!)* Prepared? Ready? Now!
el béisbol *(Ehl BEH/ees-bohl)* (the sport) baseball	**el fútbol americano** *(Ehl FOOOT-bohl Ah-meh-ree-kah-noh)* (the sport) football	**el baloncesto** *(Ehl Bah-lohn-sehs-toh)* (the sport) basketball
nadar *(nah-dahr)* to swim	**bailar** *(Bah/ee-lahr)* to dance	**correr** *(Cohr-rehr)* to run

LECCIÓN 3

Listen and sing along with this song. In Latin America, they play a game to this melody similar to "London Bridge." Have two people be the puente = bridge and catch them on the word "¡Ya!" The person caught is now part of the bridge until the next "¡Ya!"

DEPORTES = SPORTS
Melody: London Bridge   Key of C

A mí me gusta el béisbol,
el béisbol, el béisbol.
¿A tí te gusta el béisbol?
¿Preparados? ¿Listos? ¡Ya!

A mí me gusta el fútbol,
el fútbol, el fútbol.
¿A tí te gusta el fútbol?
¿Preparados? ¿Listos? ¡Ya!

A mí me gusta el fútbol americano,
fútbol americano, fútbol americano.
¿A tí te gusta el fútbol americano?
¿Preparados? ¿Listos? ¡Ya!

A mí me gusta el baloncesto,
baloncesto, baloncesto.
¿A tí te gusta el baloncesto?
¿Preparados? ¿Listos? ¡Ya!

A mí me gusta nadar,
nadar, nadar.
¿A tí te gusta nadar?
¿Preparados? ¿Listos? ¡Ya!

A mí me gusta bailar,
bailar, bailar.
¿A tí te gusta bailar?
¿Preparados? ¿Listos? ¡Ya!

A mí me gusta correr,
correr, correr.
¿A tí te gusta correr?
¿Preparados? ¿Listos? ¡Ya!

A mí me gusta un deporte,
un deporte, un deporte.
¿A tí te gusta un deporte?
¿Preparados? ¿Listos? ¡Ya!

ELEMENTARY SPANISH CHATBOOK   ©SPANISH CHAT COMPANY

LECCIÓN 3

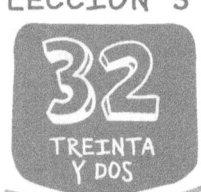

¡INTÉNTALO! = TRY IT!

CAMBIEN
A game similar to "Musical Chairs"

1. To play "Cambien" = "Change," choose one person to be the "líder = leader."
2. "Líder" stands in the middle of the circle and says, "A mí me gusta <u>nadar</u>." (or his/her favorite sport).
3. Any children that agree stand up and say, "A mí me gusta <u>nadar</u>." = I like to swim.
4. "Líder" says, "¿Preparados? ¿Listos?" = "Ready? Set?" and then claps his/her hands and says, "¡Ya!" = "Go!" This is the signal for all of the children that are standing to change to a different seat.
5. "Líder" quickly finds a seat leaving someone new without a chair. This last one = último will be the new "Líder."
6. A variation is to put a sign representing each sport in front of each child. Then when the person says, "A mí me gusta nadar," only those children with the "nadar" sign would stand.

¿PREPARADOS? ¿LISTOS? ¡YA! = READY SET? GO!

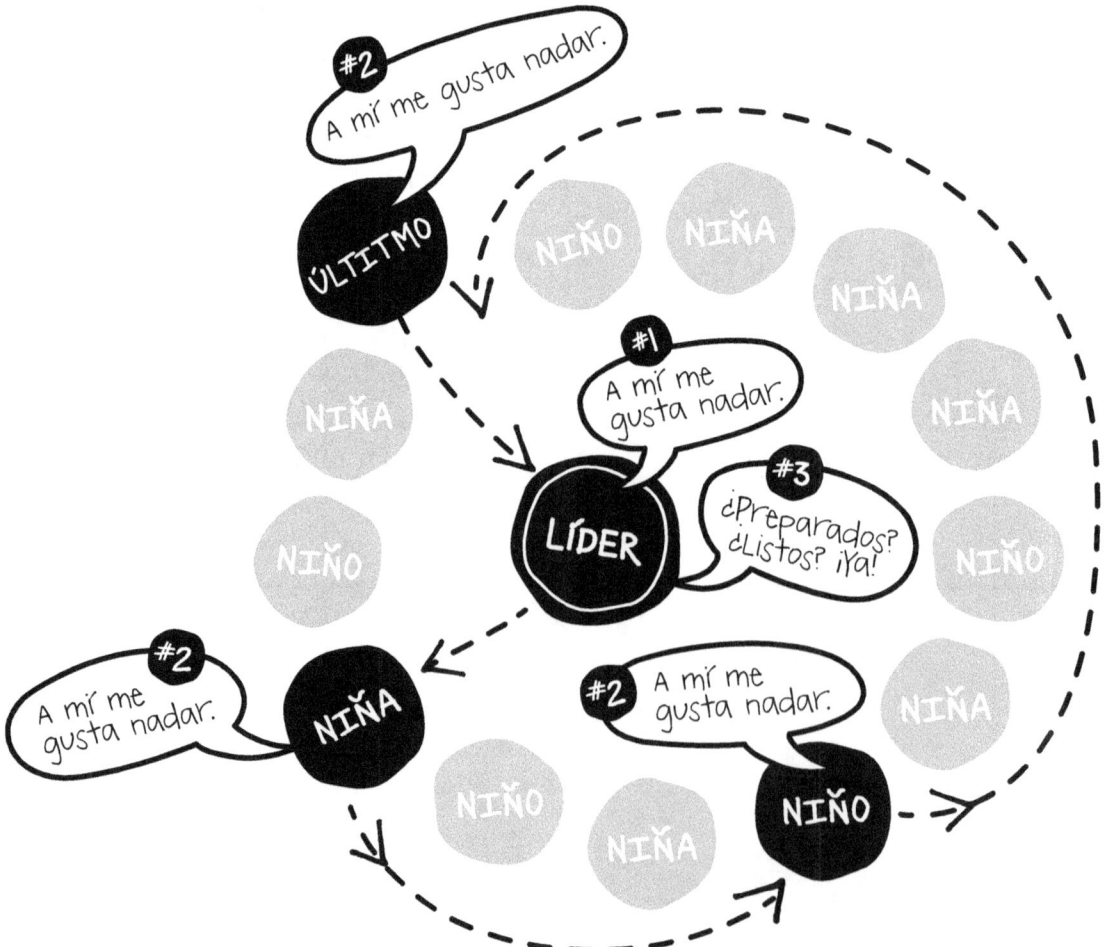

LECCIÓN 3

📖 **¡LÉELO!** = READ IT!

33
TREINTA Y TRES

Cut out the book, put the pages in order and staple them in the top left corner. Have a contest to see who can survey the most people in the next week.
 Cut out along the dashed lines

Recorta = Cut out along the dashed lines

Hola. Me llamo
_____.

(Oh-lah. Meh Yah-moh...)

Hello. My name is..

· Draw yourself doing your favorite sport.

1

Mucho gusto.

(Moo-cho Goose-toh.)

Nice to meet you.
Sign your name on the line below.

_____

_____

_____

_____

3

A mí me gusta...

(Ah MEE Meh Goose-tah ...)

I like my favorite sport.

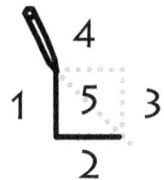

Keep track of the votes by using tally marks. In South America, some people write tally marks in a square. Start by drawing a line down and continue following the example.

5

el baloncesto   SÍ   NO
(Ehl Bah-lohn-sehs-toh)
(the sport) basketball 🏀

nadar   SÍ   NO
(Nah-dahr)
to swim

bailar   SÍ   NO
(Bah/ee-lahr)
to dance

correr   SÍ   NO
(Cohr-rehr)
to run

7

ELEMENTARY SPANISH CHATBOOK   ©SPANISH CHAT COMPANY

LECCIÓN 3

¡PRACTÍCALO! = PRACTICE IT!

Cut out the book, put the pages in order and staple them in the top left corner. Have a contest to see who can survey the most people in the next week.

Cut along the dashed lines

¿A tí te gusta un deporte?
(Ah TEE, Teh Goose-tah Oon Deh-porh-teh)

Do you like a sport?

4

¿Cómo te llamas?
(KOH-moh Teh Yah-mahs?)

What is your name?

2

¡Adiós amigos!
¡Ah-dee/OHS Ah-mee-gohs!)
Goodbye friends!

8

el béisbol
(Ehl BEH/ees-bohl)
(the sport) baseball   SÍ   NO

el fútbol
(Ehl FOOOT-bohl)
(the sport) soccer   SÍ   NO

el fútbol americano
(Ehl FOOOT-bohl Ah-meh-ree-kah-noh)
(the sport) football   SÍ   NO

6

ELEMENTARY SPANISH CHATBOOK   ©SPANISH CHAT COMPANY

¡JUÉGALO! = PLAY IT!

LECCIÓN 3

TREINTA Y CINCO

TURISTAS
A game similar to "Battleship"

1. To play "Turistas" = "Tourists," draw a tiny turista near the name of one Spanish-speaking country that you would like to visit = visitar *(Vee-see-tahr)*. Do not show your partner. For example, #1 draws a person by the word Ecuador and #2 draws a person by the word Cuba.

2. #1 says, "¿A tí te gusta visitar a Venezuela?"

3. #2 says, "No, a mí no me gusta visitar a Venezuela. ¿A tí te gusta visitar a Ecuador?"

4. #1 says, "Sí, a mí me gusta visitar a Ecuador."

5. #1 and #2 are both trying to be the first one to find the tourist.

MAPA = MAP

ELEMENTARY SPANISH CHATBOOK ©SPANISH CHAT COMPANY

LECCIÓN 3

¡MÍRALO! = LOOK AT IT!

MÉXICO

CIUDAD CAPITAL = CAPITAL CITY

LA CIUDAD DE MÉXICO, D.F. = MEXICO CITY

DINERO = MONEY

PESO

BANDERA = FLAG

VERDE | BLANCO | ROJO

WHICH ONE IS FALSE? (2 ARE TRUE, SO PUT AN X BY THE FALSE ONE)

Take a class vote. Ask each person to guess if #1, 2 or 3 is the false answer by holding up 1, 2 or 3 fingers. The answers are on p. 118 = ciento dieciocho in the back of this book.

1. Mole sauce served over chicken can either be verde = green, amarillo = yellow, negro = black or rojo = red.

2. The Aztecs had a dream that they should build Mexico City where they found an eagle holding a cactus in its mouth.

3. Chocolate = Cacao beans were used as money many years ago.

LECCIÓN 3

¡HAZLO! = DO IT!

37
TREINTA Y SIETE

CASCARONES = DECORATED EGGSHELLS

Cáscara = Eggshell. These are usually filled with confetti but can also be filled with flour, perfume or birdseed at weddings. Cascarones are mostly used in Mexico for Carnival and during Easter in the border towns. If you have one cracked over your head, it is supposed to bring good luck.

1. Push the top of a raw egg in with a spoon or your finger. Carefully make a hole about the size of a quarter.
2. Dump the egg in a bowl to use for any recipe.
3. Wash the eggshell with dishsoap or bleach and let dry.
4. Hold the eggshell on your thumb while decorating with watercolor paints, Easter egg dye or markers. Let dry.
5. Put confetti or small pieces of torn paper inside the eggshell.
6. Go outside and break these by clapping your hands together above someone's head. Have students go in order in a line so everyone gets a turn. Don't forget to sweep up the mess.

PAPEL PICADO = CHOPPED UP PAPER

Papel Picado decorations are used for many Mexican holidays including Día de los Muertos = Day of the Dead, November 1st-2nd, Christmas and Independence Day on September 16th.

1. Use a piece of colored tissue paper or any colored paper.
2. Fold in half two or three times.
3. Cut shapes or designs in each of the edges, leaving space between each cut area. This is similar to making a paper snowflake. Research to find more difficult designs and patterns.
4. Open it up and hang it by punching holes in two corners and attaching a string through the holes or by folding the top edge of each person's papel picado over a long string.

DÍAS FESTIVOS = HOLIDAYS

In Latin America many crafts and special foods are created for holidays.

- Try making some of the art projects suggested in the Días Festivos section on pages 114-116.
- Interview Hispanic families to find out what traditions they have for the holidays.
- Artesanía = hand made crafts are sold to tourists in many countries.
- Research to find more information about holidays and Hispanic crafts.

ELEMENTARY SPANISH CHATBOOK © SPANISH CHAT COMPANY

LECCIÓN 3

 ¡COCÍNALO! = COOK IT!

Try making the following recipe from Mexico:

TOSTADAS = TOASTED (FRIED TORTILLAS)

Remember that an adult will need to help you with anything hot. You may want to find a recipe for fresh guacamole or fresh salsa to top your tostadas or tacos.

TOSTADAS O TACOS

1. Compra las tostadas. = Buy the tostadas (flat fried shells) or tortillas (flat soft shells).
2. Calienta los frijoles. = Heat up the beans. You may use either refried beans, black beans or even any kind of meat.
3. Cubre la tostada con frijoles refritos. = Cover the tostada with refried beans.
4. Añade queso. = Add cheese. Use cheddar cheese, a Mexican blend or try the oaxacan cheese that melts like mozzarella.
5. Pon la lechuga sobre la tostada. = Put the lettuce on top of the tostada.
6. Pon la salsa. = Top it with salsa.
7. Pon pedazos de aguacate. = Add pieces of avocado or guacamole.
8. ¡Cómelo! = Eat it!
9. ¡Mmmm, qué rico! = How tasty!
10. ¡Buen provecho! ¡Disfruta tu tostada! = Bon appetit! Enjoy your tostada!

TORTILLAS: Circular, soft and flat, corn or wheat flatbreads usually cooked on a griddle. Machines can make 60,000 tortillas an hour.

CHIPS: Round or triangle fried corn tortillas.

TOSTADAS: Flat, circular fried corn tortillas.

TAQUITOS = LITTLE TACOS: Fried, rolled up corn tortillas with meat inside.

FLAUTAS = FLUTES: Fried, rolled up flour tortillas with meat inside, usually beef or chicken.

LECCIÓN 3

¡TERMÍNALO! = FINISH IT!

39
TREINTA Y NUEVE

CALENDARIO AZTECA = AZTEC CALENDAR

Make a personalized "Piedra del Sol / Calendario Azteca" = "Sun Stone / Aztec Calendar" by drawing yourself in the middle. Then put what you like to do in each season. Finally, choose 20 things you like to draw in each box around the outer circle. Write the name of each item in Spanish.

A MÍ ME GUSTA...

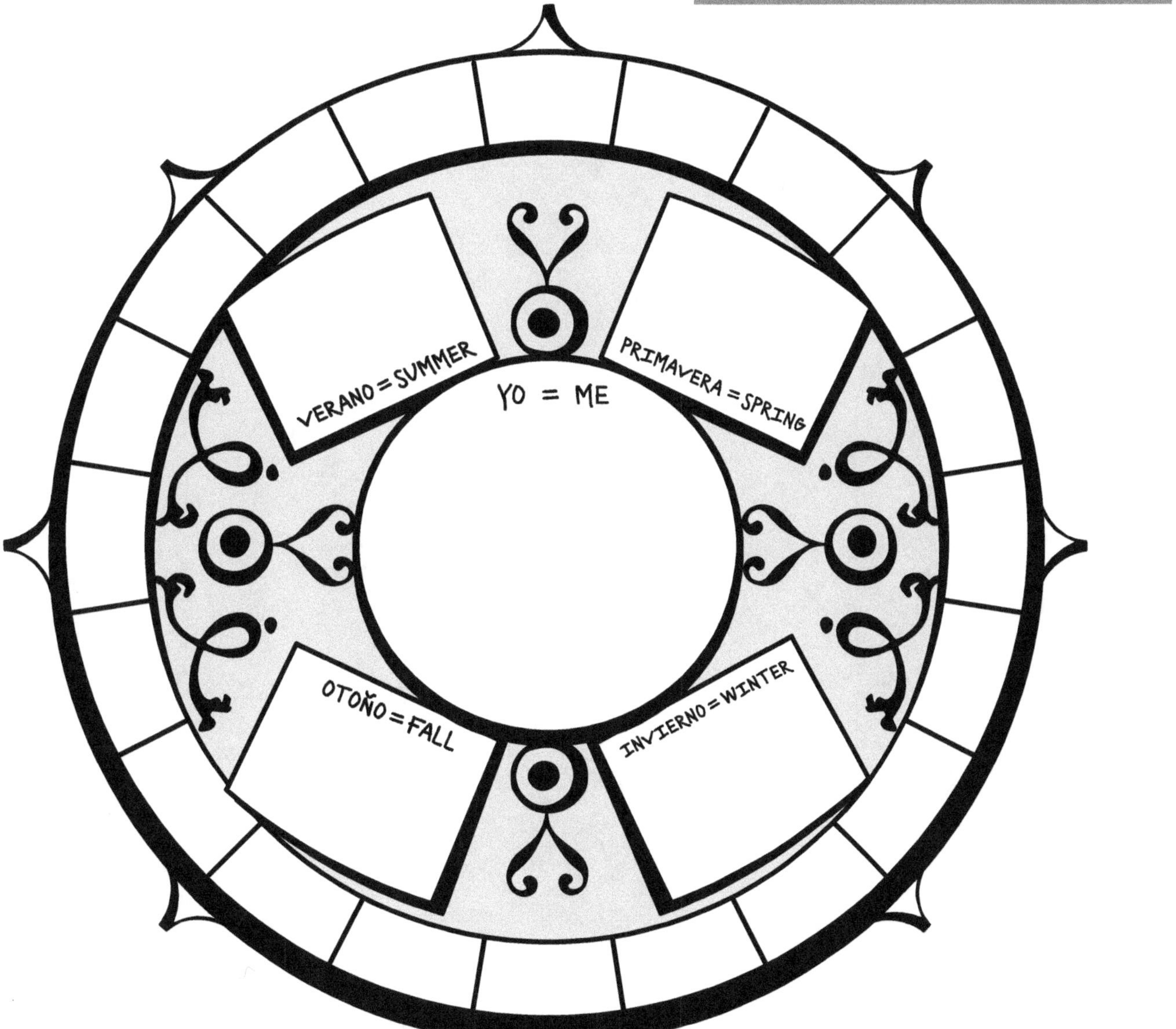

- VERANO = SUMMER
- PRIMAVERA = SPRING
- YO = ME
- OTOÑO = FALL
- INVIERNO = WINTER

LESSON 4

TENER = TO HAVE

¿CUÁNTOS AÑOS TIENES? = HOME MANY YEARS DO YOU HAVE? /HOW OLD ARE YOU?

- 🌎 Números = Numbers
- 🌎 Guatemala, El Slavador & Honduras
- 🌎 Arte = Art: Worry dolls & Volcanos
- 🌎 Comida = Food: Arroz Con Leche
- 🌎 Tarea = Homework: Mayan Math Codex

LECCIÓN 4

 ¡REPÍTELO! = REPEAT IT!

Make patterns by coloring the Spanish numbers in each row with different colors. ¡Fabuloso! = Fabulous!

COUNTING BY 1'S	COUNTING BY 1'S	COUNTING BY 10'S
0 cero *(Seh-roh)* / **1 uno** *(Oo-noh)*	**11 once** *(Ohn-seh)*	**10 diez** *(Dee/ehs)* / **100 cien** *(See/ehn)*
2 dos *(Dohs)*	**12 doce** *(Doh-seh)*	**20 veinte** *(Veh/een-teh)*
3 tres *(Trehs)*	**13 trece** *(Treh-seh)*	**30 treinta** *(Treh/een-tah)*
4 cuatro *(Qwah-troh)*	**14 catorce** *(Kah-tohr-seh)*	**40 cuarenta** *(Qwah-rent-tah)*
5 cinco *(Seen-koh)*	**15 quince** *(Keen-seh)*	**50 cincuenta** *(Seen-qwehn-tah)*
6 seis *(Seh/ace)*	**16 dieciséis** *(Dee/eh-see-seh/ace)*	**60 sesenta** *(Seh-sehn-tah)*
7 siete *(See/eh-teh)*	**17 diecisiete** *(Dee/eh-see-see/eh-teh)*	**70 setenta** *(Seh-ten-tah)*
8 ocho *(Oh-choh)*	**18 dieciocho** *(Dee/eh-see/oh-choh)*	**80 ochenta** *(Oh-chen-tah)*
9 nueve *(Noo/eh-veh)* / **10 diez** *(Dee/ehs)*	**19 diecinueve** *(Dee/eh-see-noo/eh-veh)*	**90 noventa** *(Noh-vehn-tah)*
¿Cuántos años tienes? *(KWAHN-tohs Ahn-ñyohs Tee/eh-nehs?)* How old are you / How many years do you have?	**20 veinte** *(Veh/een-teh)*	**más o menos** *(Mahs Oh Meh-nohs)* more or less
	Tengo nueve años. *(Tehn-goh Noo/eh-veh Ahn-ñyohs.)* I have / I am nine years old.	**muchos o pocos** *(Moo-chos Oh Poh-kohs)* many or few

ELEMENTARY SPANISH CHATBOOK ©SPANISH CHAT COMPANY

LECCIÓN 4

Listen and sing the numbers song. You may want to form a circle with one student in the middle using his/her index finger as a pointer. The pointer stops at the end of each verse and that person becomes the next pointer. On the right hand verses, each student can vote by raising his/her hand to indicate the answer that best fits. This song can also be used to select a student to be a helper or count students as they line up.

NÚMEROS = NUMBERS
Melody: Farmer in the Dell   Key of A

1 uno, 2 dos,
3 tres, 4 cuatro,
5 cinco, 6 seis, 7 siete,
8 ocho, 9 nueve,
y 10 diez.

11 once, 12 doce,
13 trece, 14 catorce,
15 quince, 16 dieciséis, 17 diecisiete,
18 dieciocho, 19 diecinueve,
y 20 veinte.

21 veintiuno, 22 veintidós,
23 veintitrés, 24 veinticuatro,
25 veinticinco, 26 veintiséis,
27 veintisiete,
28 veintiocho, 29 veintinueve,
y 30 treinta.

10 diez, 20 veinte,
30 treinta, 40 cuarenta,
50 cincuenta, 60 sesenta, 70 setenta,
80 ochenta, 90 noventa,
y 100 cien.

¿Cuántos años tienes?
¿Cuántos años tienes?
Tengo más de ocho años.
Tengo más de ocho.
Tengo menos de ocho años.
Tengo menos de ocho.

¿Cuántos animales tienes?
¿Cuántos animales tienes?
Tengo más de dos animales.
Tengo más de dos.
Tengo menos de dos animales.
Tengo menos de dos.

¿Cuántos libros tienes?
¿Cuántos libros tienes?
Yo tengo pocos libros.
Yo tengo pocos.
Yo tengo muchos libros.
Yo tengo muchos.

LECCIÓN 4

42 CUARENTA Y DOS

¡INTÉNTALO! = TRY IT!

MÁS O MENOS
A game similar to "Secret number"

1. To play the game "Más o Menos" = "More or Less," you will need a partner.
2. Think of a number between 1 and 100 and write it in the box below without showing your partner.
3. Take turns trying to guess the other person's number in Spanish.
4. If the guessed number is too low, the partner will say, "más."
5. If the guessed number is too high, the partner will say, "menos." Of course, all numbers guessed must be said in Spanish. For example, 12 = doce.

MENOS DE 100

← Escribes tu número secreto aquí. = Write your secret number here.

MÁS DE 1

When having a tough day, Hispanics will answer the question, "¿Cómo estás? = How are you?" with the reply, "más o menos."

ELEMENTARY SPANISH CHATBOOK © SPANISH CHAT COMPANY

LECCIÓN 4

📖 **¡LÉELO!** = READ IT!

43
CUARENTA Y TRES

Cut out these flashcards and play the "Lotería" = "Bingo" game from p. 45 = cuarenta y cinco.

Recorta = Cut out along the dashed lines ✂️

---

1 uno &
11 once
(Oo-noh &
Ohn-seh)

LECCIÓN 4

2 dos &
12 doce
(Dohs &
Doh-seh)

LECCIÓN 4

3 tres &
13 trece
(Trehs &
Treh-seh)

LECCIÓN 4

---

4 cuatro &
14 catorce
(Qwah-troh &
Kah-tohr-seh)

LECCIÓN 4

5 cinco &
15 quince
(Seen-koh &
Keen-seh)

LECCIÓN 4

6 seis &
16 dieciséis
(Seh/ace &
Dee/eh-see-seh/ace)

LECCIÓN 4

---

7 siete &
17 diecisiete
(See/eh-teh &
Dee/eh-see-see/eh-teh)

LECCIÓN 4

8 ocho &
18 dieciocho
(Oh-cho &
Dee/eh-see/oh-cho)

LECCIÓN 4

9 nueve &
19 diecinueve
(Noo/eh-veh &
Dee/eh-see-noo/eh-veh)

LECCIÓN 4

ELEMENTARY SPANISH CHATBOOK

©SPANISH CHAT COMPANY

LECCIÓN 4

¡PRACTÍCALO! = PRACTICE IT!

Play the "Lotería" = "Bingo" game from
p. 45 = cuarenta y cinco using these flashcards.

Recorta = Cut out along the dashed lines

30 treinta
(Treh/een-tah)

20 veinte
(Veh/een-teh)

**10 diez &
100 cien**
*(Dee/ehs &
See/ehn)*

60 sesenta
(Seh-sehn-tah)

50 cincuenta
(Seen-qwehn-tah)

40 cuarenta
(Qwah-rent-tah)

90 noventa
(Noh-vehn-tah)

80 ochenta
(Oh-chen-tah)

70 setenta
(Seh-ten-tah)

¡JUÉGALO! = PLAY IT!

LECCIÓN 4

45
CUARENTA Y CINCO

LOTERÍA
A game similar to "Bingo"

1. To play, "Lotería" = "Bingo," put your flashcards from this lesson in a pile and shuffle them.

2. Look at the top card in the pile and write that number in the first square. If the number is 20, then choose a number between 20-29. Do the same for 30, 40, 50, 60, 70, 80 and 90. 1-20 on the front side of the flashcards can be written as is.

3. Place that flashcard on the bottom of the pile and then write the number from the top card in the next square on the bingo board below.

4. An adult will randomly open this book and call out those two page numbers in Spanish. Whenever you hear numbers that you have, cover them with frijoles = (dried) beans or a small piece of paper.

5. The first person to get 4 in a row vertically, horizontally or diagonally wins.

FRIJOLES = BEANS

¡LOTERÍA!

The word lotería also means lottery in some countries. You may see people walking around the streets selling these tickets, hoping their numbers will be called on a certain day of the week. The unemployed, elderly and stay-at home moms get together in the neighborhood = barrio to play "Bingo" with their spare change.

ELEMENTARY SPANISH CHATBOOK   ©SPANISH CHAT COMPANY

LECCIÓN 4

46
CUARENTA Y SEIS

¡MÍRALO! = LOOK AT IT!

AMÉRICA CENTRAL

GUATEMALA | HONDURAS | EL SALVADOR

CIUDAD CAPITAL = CAPITAL CITY

LA CIUDAD DE GUATEMALA	TEGUCIGALPA	SAN SALVADOR

DINERO = MONEY

QUETZAL	LEMPIRA	DÓLAR

BANDERA = FLAG

Guatemala flag: AZUL CLARO / BLANCO / AZUL CLARO	Honduras flag: AZUL CLARO / BLANCO (with 5 stars) / AZUL CLARO	El Salvador flag: AZUL CLARO / BLANCO / AZUL CLARO

WHICH ONE IS FALSE? (2 ARE TRUE, SO PUT AN X BY THE FALSE ONE)

Take a class vote. Ask each person to guess if #1, 2 or 3 is the false answer by holding up 1, 2 or 3 fingers. The answers are on p. 118 = ciento dieciocho in the back of this book.

1. The five stars on the flag of Honduras represent the five official holidays celebrated in Honduras, one of which is Children's Day, September 10.
2. Tikal, Guatemala was a large Mayan city that included 3,000 structures.
3. In "Sopa de Pata" in El Salvador, you may find yucca, plantains, corn, green beans, lemon juice, cow's stomach and cow's feet.

ELEMENTARY SPANISH CHATBOOK ©SPANISH CHAT COMPANY

LECCIÓN 4

 **¡HAZLO!** = DO IT!

47
CUARENTA Y SIETE

MUÑECAS QUITAPENAS = WORRY DOLLS

Some Guatemalans believe that if you tell your worries to these dolls at bedtime, things will be better in the morning.

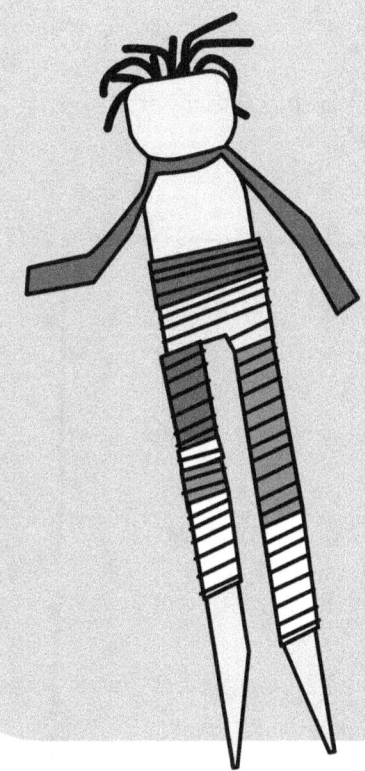

1. Use a rounded clothespin (also called a doll pin).
2. Wrap a twist tie around the neck and bend for arms.
3. Wrap different colors of yarn around the legs and arms for clothing. It is also fun to cut clothing out of wrapping paper.
4. Use a permanent marker to draw a face on the doll.
5. Add hair made from yarn or string. Make a whole family.
6. Make a casa = house out of small paper bag gluing on grass, sticks and/or toothpicks to make it look like a hut.
7. Tell your doll your worries and place him/her under your pillow. Hopefully you will be worry-free very soon.

VOLCÁN = VOLCANO

Central America has many volcanoes but only ten or so are active. Night is the best time to see the glowing lava.

1. Make enough play dough for each student to have a baseball size glob. You may also purchase craft clay.
2. Turn a small 3 oz. plastic cup upside down in a 10 oz. bowl.
3. Mold the clay around the cup leaving a small gumball size opening at the top of the volcano. Let it dry and then paint it or decorate it with small people and trees.
4. Pour baking soda to fill up the hole (approx. 2 Tablespoons)
5. Now mix a few drops of red food coloring with 1/2 cup of white vinegar per volcano. Pour it in the hole and watch the lava erupt. Repeat for further fun.

PLASTALINA = PLAY DOUGH

- 2 tazas harina = 2 cups flour
- 2 cucaradas aceite = 2 Tablespoons vegetable oil
- 2 cucaradas cremor tártaro = 2 Tablespoons cream of tartar
- 2 tazas agua con 1/2 taza sal = Dissolve 1/2 cup salt in 2 cups boiling water
- Mézclalo = Mix it together

ELEMENTARY SPANISH CHATBOOK ©SPANISH CHAT COMPANY

LESSON 4

48 CUARENTA Y OCHO

¡COCÍNALO! = COOK IT!

Try making the following recipe popular throughout Latin America:

PASTEL DE TRES LECHES = THREE MILK CAKE

Remember that an adult will need to help you with anything hot. This is a simplified version to use with kids in a classroom. Research to find more authentic recipes.

PASTEL DE TRES LECHES

1. <u>Hornea las magdalenas.</u> = Bake the cupcakes. You will need one white cupcake per student.

2. <u>Dale un palillo.</u> = Give a toothpick and a cupcake to each student.

3. <u>Cuenta hasta 20.</u> = Count to 20 in Spanish while making 20 holes in the cupcake.

4. <u>Mezcla las tres leches.</u> = Mix the three milks. For 24 cupcakes, mix 1/2 can of sweetened condensed milk with 1/2 can of evaporated milk and 2 cups of whipped cream. This is your "Tres leches" mixture.

5. <u>Pon las tres leches encima de las magdalenas.</u> = Put (pour) the three milk mixture on top of each cupcake. You may want to put the cupcake into a bowl or deep dish.

6. <u>Usa la crema batida arriba de todo.</u> = Use the whipped cream on top of everything. This will cover the holes like frosting.

7. <u>Enfríalo.</u> = Chill it. Put in the fridge overnight if possible. If not, just eat it immediately with a spoon.

8. <u>¡Cómelo!</u> = Eat it!

9. <u>¡Mmmm, qué rico!</u> = How tasty!

10. <u>¡Buen provecho! Disfruta tu pastel de tres leches.</u> = Enjoy your three milk cake.

PUERTO RICO AND CUBA: Cream of coconut is sometimes substituted for the sweetened condensed milk.

GUATEMALA, NICARAGUA AND MEXICO: Sometimes other ingredients such as chocolate, fruits or nuts are added.

4 LECHES: To make a four milk cake, add "cajeta" which is a thick syrup made from caramelized sweetened condensed milk.

VOLCANO: To make a volcano snack, bite the end off of a pointed ice cream cone. Turn it upside down in a bowl. Add chocolate ice cream into the hole and then pour lava (strawberry syrup) down the sides.

¡TERMÍNALO! = FINISH IT!

CÓDIGO MAYA = MAYAN CODE

One of the great Pre-Columbian civilizations was the Mayan Empire. Math is one area in which they made many contributions. The Mayans were the first people to use the concept of zero. Zero was depicted in the Mayan writing system with a drawing of a seashell. The Mayan numbers 1–19 were originally formed by using sticks and stones. Write simple Mayan math problems using sticks (lines) and stones (dots) instead of numbers. You may also use the English alphabetical letters to write coded messages to your amigos = friends. Bring at least two sentences and two math problems for your friends to decode at the beginning of the next class. Remember that the pronunciation of the Spanish alphabet is on page 11 = once of this book.

0	1	2	3	4	5	6	7	8	9
A	B	C	D	E	F	G	H	I	

10	11	12	13	14	15	16	17	18	19
J	K	L	M	N	Ñ	O	P	Q	R

20	21	22	23	24	25	26	27
S	T	U	V	W	X	Y	Z

LECCIÓN 5 LESSON

DECIR = TO SAY

¿CÓMO DICES... EN ESPAÑOL? = HOW DO YOU SAY...IN SPANISH?

- 🌎 Familia = Family
- 🌎 Nicaragua, Costa Rica & Panama
- 🌎 Arte = Art: Mola & Ox Cart wheel
- 🌎 Comida = Food: Gallo Pinto
- 🌎 Tarea = Homework: Family Project

LECCIÓN 5

50 CINCUENTA — ¡REPÍTELO! = REPEAT IT!

Draw a picture to illustrate each word or phrase. Repeat them in Spanish. ¡Excelente! = Excellent!

¿Cómo dices, "what a great family," en español?
(Koh-moh Dee-sehs... Ehn Ehs-pah-ñyohl?)
How do you say...in Spanish?

Yo digo, "¡qué buena familia!"
(Yoh Dee-goh, "¡KEH Boo/eh-nah Fah-mee-lee/ah!")
I say, "what a great family!"

La mamá dice "te quiero."
(Lah Mah-MAH Dee-seh "Teh Kee/eh-roh")
The mom says, "I love you."

El papá dice, "de nada."
(Ehl Pah-PAH Dee-seh "Deh Nah-dah.")
The dad says, "you're welcome."

La hermana dice, "muchas gracias."
(Lah Ehr-mah-nah Dee-seh, "Moo-chahs Grah-see/ahs.")
The sister says, "thank you very much."

El hermano dice, "¡vámonos!"
(Ehl Ehr-mah-noh Dee-seh, "VAH-moh-nohs!")
The brother says, "let's go!"

Los abuelos dicen, "bienvenidos."
(Lohs Ah-boo/eh-lohs Dee-sen, "Bee/ehn-veh-nee-dohs.")
The grandparents say, "welcome."

El perro dice, "guau, guau." La gata dice, "miau, miau."
(Ehl Peh-roh Dee-seh, "Woo/ah/oo, Woo/au/oo." Lah Gah-tah Dee-seh, "Mee-ah/oo, Mee-ah/oo.")
The male dog says, "bow-wow." The female cat says, "meow, meow."

La casa no dice nada. Silencio, por favor.
(Lah Kah-sah Noh Dee-seh Nah-dah. See-lehn-see/oh Pohr Fah-vohr.)
The house says nothing. Silence, please.

ELEMENTARY SPANISH CHATBOOK ©Spanish Chat Company

¡Cántalo! = Sing it!

LECCIÓN 5

51
CINCUENTA Y UNO

Listen and sing the family song. This is similar to the song, "Father Abraham" where you add an action on after every verse. Use sign language or make up a sign for each of the verses. By the end of the song, "mi casa no dice nada," = my house is silent.

FAMILIA = FAMILY
Melody: Un Elefante   Key of C

Mi mamá dice, mi mamá dice,
"Te quiero. Te quiero."
Yo digo, "¡qué buena,
qué buena familia!"

Mi papá dice, mi papá dice,
"De nada. De nada."
"Te quiero. Te quiero."
"¡Qué buena familia!"

Mi hermana dice, mi hermana dice,
"Muchas gracias. Muchas gracias."
"De nada. De nada."
"Te quiero. Te quiero."
"¡Qué buena familia!"

Mi hermano dice, mi hermano dice,
"¡Vámonos! ¡Vámonos!"
"Muchas gracias. Muchas gracias."
"De nada. De nada."
"Te quiero. Te quiero."
"¡Qué buena familia!"

Mis abuelos dicen, mis abuelos
dicen, "Bienvenidos. Bienvenidos."
"¡Vámonos! ¡Vámonos!"
"Muchas gracias. Muchas gracias."
"De nada. De nada."
"Te quiero. Te quiero."
"¡Qué buena familia!"

Mi gata dice, mi gata dice,
"Miau, miau, miau, miau,
miau, miau, miau, miau."
"Bienvenidos. Bienvenidos."
"¡Vámonos! ¡Vámonos!"
"Muchas gracias. Muchas gracias."
"De nada. De nada."
"Te quiero. Te quiero."
"¡Qué buena familia!"

Mi perro dice, mi perro dice,
"Guau, guau, guau guau,
guau, guau, guau, guau."
"Miau, miau, miau, miau,
miau, miau, miau, miau."
"Bienvenidos. Bienvenidos."
"¡Vámonos! ¡Vámonos!"
"Muchas gracias. Muchas gracias."
"De nada. De nada."
"Te quiero. Te quiero."
"¡Qué buena familia!"

Mi casa no dice nada,
no dice nada.
Mi casa no dice nada.
Silencio, por favor.
Silencio, por favor.

ELEMENTARY SPANISH CHATBOOK   ©SPANISH CHAT COMPANY

LECCIÓN 5

¡INTÉNTALO! = TRY IT!

DIGO UN NÚMERO
A new game called, "I Say a Number"

1. To play "Digo un número" = "I Say a Number," you will need to divide into two lines.

2. Write the numerals 0-9 on big signs. You will need one set for each line. Divide these signs between the players in each line. You may have one or more per player depending on the size of your class. If you have more than 20 students, then leave all of the numbers on a table and have the first two players in each line grab the numbers they need as you say each number.

3. As soon as the teams are lined up with their signs, the teacher says a number between 1 and 100 and the first team to make the correct number wins an extra point. For example, "Yo digo ochenta y uno" The players holding #8 and #1 would have to get together in the back of the room facing the teacher to make the number 81. If the black team did it first, they would get two points—one point for being correct and one point for being first. The white team would only get one point for being correct.

4. To make this more difficult, call out math equations such as 20-4 = ? The first team to make 16 would win a point.

5. The team with the most points wins.

MATEMÁTICAS = MATH

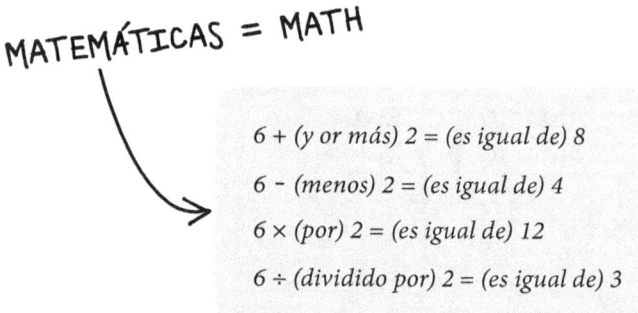

6 + (y or más) 2 = (es igual de) 8
6 − (menos) 2 = (es igual de) 4
6 × (por) 2 = (es igual de) 12
6 ÷ (dividido por) 2 = (es igual de) 3

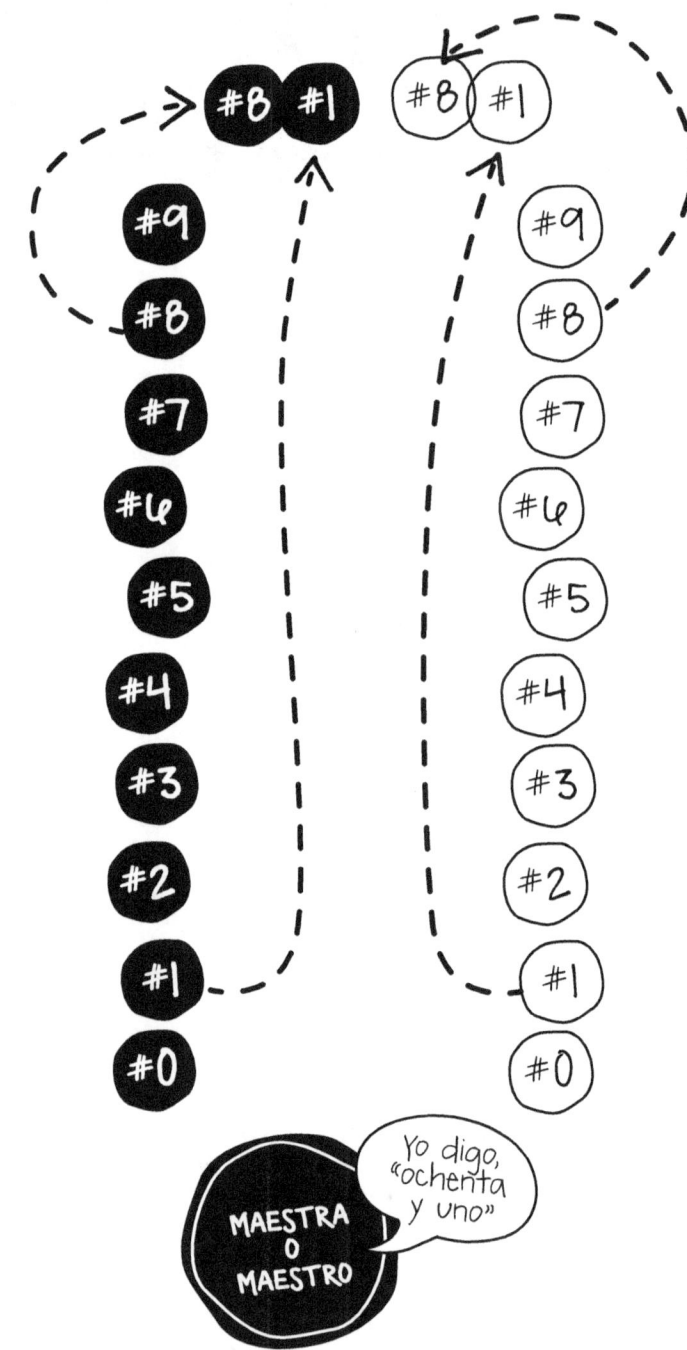

LECCIÓN 5

 **¡LÉELO!** = READ IT!

53
CINCUENTA Y TRES

Cut out these flashcards and play the "Toma Todo" = "Take Everything" game from p. 55 = cincuenta y cinco.

Recorta = Cut out along the dashed lines

¿Cómo dices, "what a great family," en español?
(Koh-moh Dee-sehs... Ehn Ehs-pah-ñyohl?)

LECCIÓN 5

Yo digo, "¡qué buena familia!"
(Yoh Dee-goh, "¡KEH Boo/eh-nah Fah-mee-lee/ah!")

LECCIÓN 5

La mamá dice "te quiero."
(Lah Mah-MAH Dee-seh "Teh Kee/eh-roh.")

LECCIÓN 5

El papá dice, "de nada."
(Ehl Pah-PAH Dee-seh "Deh Nah-dah.")

LECCIÓN 5

La hermana dice, "muchas gracias."
(Lah Ehr-mah-nah Dee-seh, "Moo-chahs Grah-see/ahs.")

LECCIÓN 5

El hermano dice, "¡Vámonos!""
(Ehl Ehr-mah-noh Dee-seh, "VAH-moh-nohs!")

LECCIÓN 5

Los abuelos dicen, "bienvenidos."
(Lohs Ah-boo/eh-lohs Dee-sen, "Bee/ehn-veh-nee-dohs.")

LECCIÓN 5

El perro dice, "guau, guau." La gata dice, "miau, miau."
(Ehl Peh-roh Dee-she, "Woo/ah/oo, Woo/au/oo." Lah Gah-tah Dee-she, "Mee-ah/oo, Mee-ah/oo.")

LECCIÓN 5

La casa no dice nada. Silencio, por favor.
(Lah Kah-sah Noh Dee-seh Nah-dah. See-lehn-see/oh, Pohr Fah-vohr.)

LECCIÓN 5

ELEMENTARY SPANISH CHATBOOK   ©SPANISH CHAT COMPANY

LECCIÓN 5

¡PRACTÍCALO! = PRACTICE IT!

Play the "Toma Todo" "Take Everything" game from p. 55 = cincuenta y cinco using these flashcards.

Recorta = Cut out along the dashed lines

The mom says, "I love you."

I say, "what a great family!"

How do you say "what a great family," in Spanish?

The brother says, "let's go!"

The sister says, "thank you very much."

The dad says, "you're welcome."

The house says nothing. Silence, please.

The male dog says, "bow-wow." The female cat says, "meow, meow."

The grandparents say, "welcome."

ELEMENTARY SPANISH CHATBOOK ©SPANISH CHAT COMPANY

¡JUÉGALO! = PLAY IT!

LECCIÓN 5
CINCUENTA Y CINCO

TOMA TODO

A game similar to playing with marbles and jacks.

To play "Toma Todo" = "Take Everything," each player chooses six flashcards. Either play this game in partners, groups of three or two big teams. Student #1 will roll the dice and follow the directions below then give the dice to Student #2. The first person to run out of flashcards loses the game. Note: If you roll a Toma and there are no flashcards in the middle then your turn is over and the next person rolls.

IF YOU ROLL A 1, TOMA 1 = TAKE 1
You take one from the center and say it in Spanish.

TOMA = TAKE

IF YOU ROLL A 2, TOMA 2 = TAKE 2
You take two from the center and say them in Spanish.

IF YOU ROLL A 3, PON 1 = PUT 1
You put one in the center and say it in Spanish.

IF YOU ROLL A 4, PON 2 = PUT 2
You put two in the center and say it in Spanish.

PON = PUT

IF YOU ROLL A 5, TODOS PONEN = EVERYONE PUTS ONE
Each player has to put one into the center and say it in Spanish.

IF YOU ROLL A 6, *TOMA TODO* = TAKE EVERYTHING
¡Jackpot! Take all the pieces from the center and as an extra bonus, you don't have to say anything.

LECCIÓN 5

 ¡MÍRALO! = LOOK AT IT!

AMÉRICA CENTRAL

NICARAGUA | COSTA RICA | PANAMÁ

CIUDAD CAPITAL = CAPITAL CITY

NICARAGUA	COSTA RICA	PANAMÁ
MANAGUA	SAN JOSÉ	LA CIUDAD DE PANAMÁ

DINERO = MONEY

CÓRDOBA	COLÓN	DÓLAR/BALBOA

BANDERA = FLAG

Nicaragua flag: AZUL CLARO / BLANCO / AZUL CLARO

Costa Rica flag: AZUL / BLANCO / ROJO / BLANCO / AZUL

Panamá flag: BLANCO (with AZUL star) / ROJO / AZUL / BLANCO (with ROJO star)

WHICH ONE IS FALSE? (2 ARE TRUE, SO PUT AN X BY THE FALSE ONE)

Take a class vote. Ask each person to guess if #1, 2 or 3 is the false answer by holding up 1, 2 or 3 fingers. The answers are on p. 118 = ciento dieciocho in the back of this book.

○ **1.** 1. On a clear night you see the lava balls cascading down the active Volcano Arenal in Costa Rica. By day it is fun to swim in the natural hot springs.

○ **2.** 2. Lago = Lake Nicaragua is called "Mar Dulce" = Sweet Sea. It is a freshwater lake with tuna fish and sharks.

○ **3.** 3. It takes large ships about two hours to cross the Panama Canal.

LECCIÓN 5

 ¡HAZLO! = DO IT!

57
CINCUENTA Y SIETE

MOLAS CON TUS NOMBRES = QUILT "CLOTHING" WITH YOUR NAMES

Mola means clothing in the Kuna language spoken on the islands extending from Panama to Colombia. A mola is stiched like a quilt with many colors.

1. Write your name on a piece of construction paper.

2. Circle around your name with many various colors and finish when you reach the edge of the paper.

3. For a more difficult mola pattern, draw the shape of an animal on the top piece of paper. Now carefully cut out some designs and glue other colors of paper behind your original animal.

RUEDAS DE CARRETAS = OX CART WHEELS

The ox carts in Costa Rica are hand painted and were used to transport coffee beans. Many families have their own designs, like a family crest.

1. Cut a large circle out of paper to design your own ox cart wheel. Use lots of different colors and patterns. Research different designs used in Costa Rica. What symbols would you use to represent your family?

2. You could make a cart by designing four wheels out of cardstock paper. Decorate the bottom half of a box. Good boxes for this are the boxes containing checks or processed cheese. Attach the wheels using brads with two prongs. Make a handle with a pencil. Glue on real coffee beans to make it look authentic.

LECCIÓN 5

 **¡COCÍNALO!** = COOK IT!

Try making the following recipe popular in Nicaragua and Costa Rica:

GALLO PINTO = SPOTTED ROOSTER (BEANS AND RICE)

Remember that an adult will need to help you with anything hot. There is no chicken in this recipe, some say the name comes from the spotted appearance of the rice when cooked with the beans.

GALLO PINTO

1. Cocina 2 tazas de arroz. = Cook 2 cups of rice.
2. Pica 1 cebolla blanca y dos dientes de ajo. = Chop 1 white onion and two cloves of garlic.
3. Fríelos en 1 cucharada de aceite de oliva. = Fry in 1 Tablespoon of olive oil. (Be careful to not burn it.)
4. Mezcla con 1 lata de frijoles negros. = Mix in 1 can of black beans. Do not drain the beans.
5. Añade el arroz cocido. = Add the cooked rice.
6. Añade 1 cucharadita de salsa inglesa. = Add 1 teaspoon of worcestershire sauce
7. Pon una pizca de chiles molidos. = Put dash or two of crushed red pepper.
8. Cocínalo por 5 minutos. = Cook it for 5 minutes.
9. ¡Cómelo! = Eat it! ¡Mmmm, qué rico! = How tasty!
10. ¡Buen provecho! Disfruta tu gallo pinto. = Bon appetit! Enjoy your beans and rice.

NICARAGUA AND HONDURAS: They use red beans instead of black beans.

PUERTO RICO AND DOMINICAN REPUBLIC A similar dish is made with kidney beans or pigeon peas.

SPAIN AND CUBA: This dish is called "moros y cristianos" = Moors and Christians.

PANAMA AND EL SALVADOR A similar dish is called casamiento = marriage ceremony.

PARA DESAYUNO = FOR BREAKFAST: Gallo pinto is served in Costa Rica along with scrambled eggs. This may be the only meal the coffee farmers eat all day long.

LECCIÓN 5

🏠 ¡TERMÍNALO! = FINISH IT!

EL PROYECTO DE LA FAMILIA = THE FAMILY PROJECT

Bring in a family photo and describe your family in Spanish or draw a family tree and label your family members in Spanish. Another idea is to make paper dolls for each of your family members. You may draw your family tree or write your project on the back of this page. To help you fill in the blanks below, use the glosario = glossary pp. 122-137 = ciento veintidós hasta ciento treinta y siete. Present your family project at the beginning of the next class.

Ejemplos = Examples:

> **1. Me llamo Julia. Yo estoy feliz. Yo tengo 41 años. Yo digo, "me gusta viajar." =**
> My name is Julie. I am happy. I am 41 years old. I say, "I like to travel."
>
> **2. Mi hermano se llama Andrew. Él está bien. Él tiene 25 años. Él dice, "me gusta esquiar." =**
> My brother is named Andrew. He is well. He is 25 years old. He says, "I like to ski."

1. Me llamo _____ (name). Yo estoy _____ (how you feel).

Yo tengo ___ (#) años. Yo digo, "me gusta _____ (something you like)."

2. Mi _____ (family member / friend) se llama _____ (name). Ella /Él está _____ (how he/she feels).

Ella /Él tiene ___ (#) años. Ella /Él dice, "me gusta _____ (something he/she likes)."

3. Mi _____ (family member / friend) se llama _____ (name). Ella/Él está _____ (how he/she feels).

Ella /Él tiene ___ (#) años. Ella /Él dice, "me gusta _____ (something he/she likes)."

ELEMENTARY SPANISH CHATBOOK   ©SPANISH CHAT COMPANY

LECCIÓN 6 LESSON

SER = TO BE

¿CUÁNDO ES TU CUMPLEAÑOS? = WHEN IS YOUR BIRTHDAY?

- 🌏 Calendario = Calendar:
    Weekdays, Months Of The Year
- 🌏 Colombia, Venezuela & Ecuador
- 🌏 Arte = Art: Gold jewelry & Rainsticks
- 🌏 Comida = Food: Tres Leches Cake
- 🌏 Tarea = Homework: A Spanish Calendar

LECCIÓN 6

¡REPÍTELO! = REPEAT IT!

Draw what you like about each month or day. Repeat them in Spanish. ¡Perfecto! = Perfect!

MESES = MONTHS	MESES = MONTHS	DÍAS DE LA SEMANA = DAYS OF THE WEEK
enero (Eh-neh-roh) January	**julio** (Who-lee/oh) July	**lunes** (Loo-nehs) Monday
febrero (Fehb-reh-roh) February	**agosto** (Ah-gohs-toh) August	**martes** (Mahr-tehs) Tuesday
marzo (Mahr-zoh) March	**septiembre** (Sehp-tee/ehm-breh) September	**miércoles** (Mee/EHR-Koh-lehs) Wednesday
abril (Ah-breel) April	**octubre** (Oct-too-breh) October	**jueves** (Who/eh-vehs) Thursday
mayo (Mah-yoh) May	**noviembre** (Noh-vee/ehm-breh) November	**viernes** (Vee/ehr-nehs) Friday
junio (Who-nee/oh) June	**diciembre** (Dee-see/ehm-breh) December	**sábado** (SAH-bah-doh) Saturday
¿Qué día es hoy? (Keh DEE-ah Ehs Oh/ee?) What day is today?	**Hoy es el 27 de diciembre.** (Oh/ee Ehs Ehl Veh/een-teh Ee See/eh-teh Deh Dee-see/ehm-breh.) Today is the 27 of December.	**domingo** (Doh-meen-goh) Sunday
¿Cuándo es tu cumpleaños? (Kwahn-doh Ehs Too Coom-pleh-ahn-ñyohs?) When is your birthday?	**Mi cumpleaños es el 15 de marzo.** (Mee Coom-pleh-ahn-ñyohs Ehs Ehl Keen-seh Deh Mahr-zoh.) My birthday is the 15 of March.	¿Qué mes es ahora? (Keh Mehs Ehs Ah-or-rah) What month is it now?

ELEMENTARY SPANISH CHATBOOK

©Spanish Chat Company

LECCIÓN 6

61
SESENTA Y UNO

Listen and sing the calendar song. You may want to march around the room as you sing and freeze when you hear today's day of the week and month of the year. You could jump up out of your seat when you hear the correct day and month. Fantástico. = Fantastic.

CALENDARIO = CALENDAR
Melody: Mary Had a Little Lamb   Key of D

¿Qué día es hoy,
es hoy, es hoy?
¿Qué día es hoy,
en el calendario?

domingo, lunes, martes,
miércoles, jueves,
viernes o sábado,
¿Qué día es hoy?

¿Cuál es tu día favorito,
favorito, favorito?
¿Cuál es tu día favorito,
en el calendario?

domingo, lunes, martes,
miércoles, jueves,
viernes o sábado,
¿Cuál es tu día favorito?

¿Qué mes es ahora,
es ahora, es ahora?
¿Qué mes es ahora,
en el calendario?

enero, febrero, marzo, abril,
mayo, junio, julio,
agosto, septiembre, octubre,
noviembre o diciembre.

¿Cuándo es tu cumpleaños,
cumpleaños, cumpleaños?
¿Cuándo es tu cumpleaños,
en el calendario?

enero, febrero, marzo, abril,
mayo, junio, julio,
agosto, septiembre, octubre,
noviembre o diciembre.

ELEMENTARY SPANISH CHATBOOK   ©SPANISH CHAT COMPANY

LECCIÓN 6

¡INTÉNTALO! = TRY IT!

¡BUENA SUERTE!
A game similar to the rollar skating game using giant dice

1. To play "Buena Suerte" = "Good Luck," you will need two dice.

2. To set up the game, write the 12 months of the year in Spanish on 11 slips of paper and hang them around the room. For example, write 1 = enero/2 = febrero, 3 = marzo, 4= abril... You will need to combine enero and febrero on the same sign because it is impossible to roll a 1 using two dice.

3. Students have until the end of the months of the year song to choose a spot around the room.

4. Give the dice to one student and say, "tiras los dados" = "throw/roll the dice." Now add the number on both dice. For example, if you roll a 1 = uno and a 3 = tres it would be 4 = cuatro. Everyone at 4 = abril would have to go sit down.

5. Roll again and if it is an 8, the people in 8 = agosto would be out.

6. Keep rolling until one student is left at the final winning month. ¡Buena suerte!

7. Start again with all of the students and give them until the end of the months of the year song to find their "lucky" month.

TIRAS LOS DADOS. = THROW THE DICE.

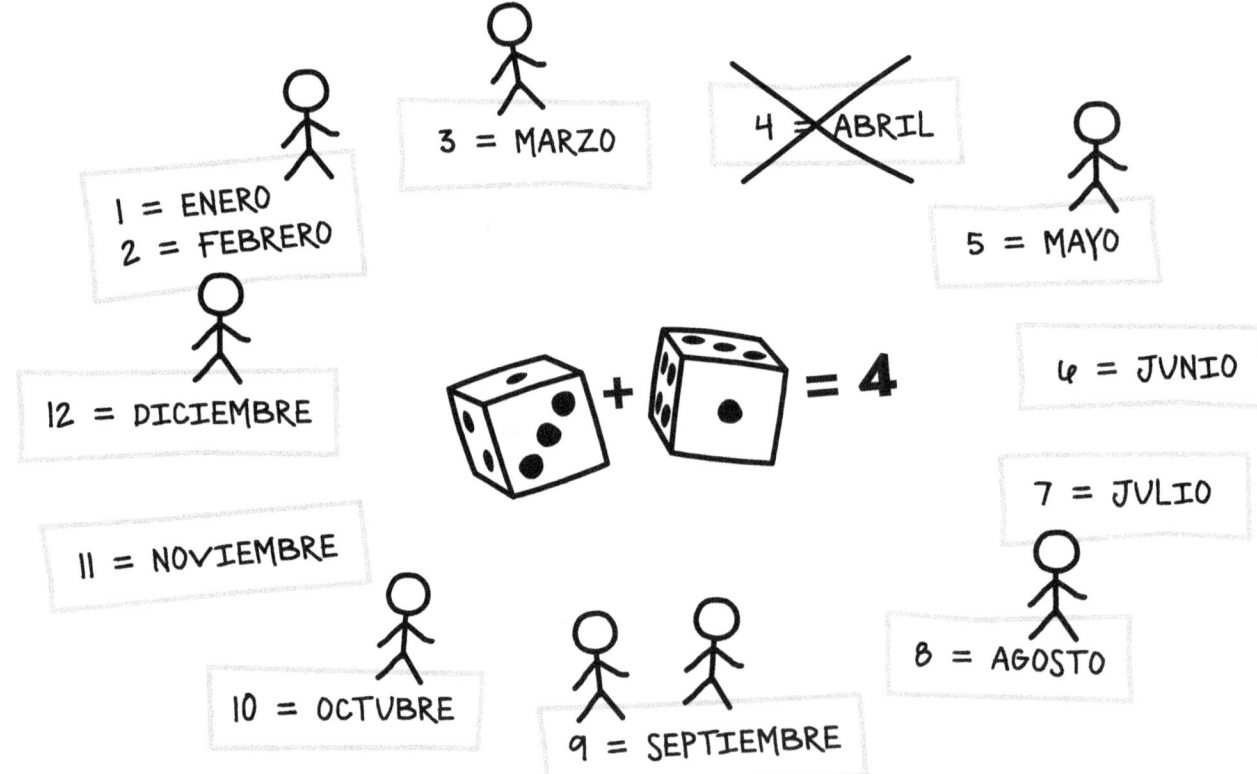

ELEMENTARY SPANISH CHATBOOK ©SPANISH CHAT COMPANY

¡LÉELO! = READ IT!

LECCIÓN 6
63 SESENTA Y TRES

Cut out the book, put the pages in order and staple them them in the top left corner.
Have a contest to see who can survey the most people in the next week.

Buenos días.
(Bwehn-ohs DEE-ahs.)
Good morning.

Buenas tardes.
(Bwehn-ahs Tahr-dehs.)
Good afternoon/evening.

Buenas noches.
(Bwehn-ahs Noh-chehs.)
Good night.

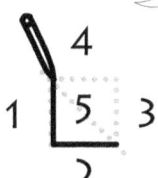

Is it morning, noon or night? Ask your listener about his/her birthday and the date today. use tally marks to keep track like they do in South America. Start by drawing a line down and continue following the example.

Recorta = Cut out along the dashed lines

1

¿Cuándo es tu cumpleaños?
(Kwahn-doh Ehs Too Coom-pleh-ahn-ñyohs?)
When is your birthday?

Mi cumpleaños es en...
(Mee Coom-pleh-ahn-ñyohs Ehs Ehn...)
My birthday is in...

3

julio
(Who-lee/oh) July

agosto
(Ah-gohs-toh) August

septiembre
(Sehp-tee/ehm-breh) September

octubre
(Oct-too-breh) October

noviembre
(No-vee/ehm-breh) November

diciembre
(Dee-see/ehm-breh) December

5

jueves
(Who/eh-vehs)
Thursday

viernes
(Vee/ehr-nehs)
Friday

sábado
(SAH-bah-doh)
Saturday

domingo
(Doh-meen-goh)
Sunday

7

ELEMENTARY SPANISH CHATBOOK ©SPANISH CHAT COMPANY

LECCIÓN 6

¡PRACTÍCALO! = PRACTICE IT!

Cut out this book and staple it. Have a contest to see who can read it to the most people this week.

Recorta = Cut out along the dashed lines

enero
(Eh-neh-roh) January

febrero
(Fehb-reh-roh) February

marzo
(Mahr-zoh) March

abril
(Ah-breel) April

mayo
(Mah-yoh) May

junio
(Who-nee/oh) June

4

¿Cómo te llamas?
(KOH-moh Teh Yah-mahs?)
What is your name?

Me llamo...
(Meh Yah-moh...)
My name is...
Sign your name on the line below.

_____

_____

_____

2

¡Adiós amigos!
(¡Ah-dee/OHS Ah-mee-gohs!)
Goodbye friends!

Hasta _____
    (día de la semana)
(Ahs-tah...)
See you on...(day of the week)

8

¿Qué día es hoy?
(Keh Dee-ah Ehs Oh/ee?) What day is today?

Hoy es...
(Oh/ee Ehs...) Today is...

lunes
(Loo-nehs)
Monday

martes
(Mahr-tehs)
Tuesday

miércoles
(Mee-EHR-koh-lehs)
Wednesday

6

ELEMENTARY SPANISH CHATBOOK   ©SPANISH CHAT COMPANY

LECCIÓN 6

¡JUÉGALO! = PLAY IT!

65 SESENTA Y CINCO

DIBUJOS
A game similar to "Pictionary"

EQUIPO = TEAM

1. To play "Dibujos" = "Drawings," divide the class into dos equipos = two teams.

2. Choose one Spanish word from any flashcard or, to make it more difficult, use the glosario = glossary pp. 122-137 = ciento veintidós hasta ciento treinta y seis.

3. One person from each team illustrates the Spanish word in front of their team without talking or making noises. They can use acciones = actions like charades or drawings like Pictionary.

4. Each equipo = team shouts out answers trying to be the first one to guess correctly. A quieter and calmer variation is to give a white board to each team and the first person to spell the answer correctly gets a point. Pass the whiteboards around so everyone gets a chance to be the writer.

5. The team with the most points wins.

6. The first person to guess the correct word wins.

Teatros = theaters and Cines = movie theaters are great forms of entertainment in Latin America. Bailes Folklóricos = Folkloric dances. Most countries have traditional forms of dancing with elaborate costumes. Find information about famous actors, singers and dancers from Latin America. Draw a picture of your favorite costume.

ELEMENTARY SPANISH CHATBOOK ©SPANISH CHAT COMPANY

LECCIÓN 6

66
SESENTA Y SEIS

¡MÍRALO! = LOOK AT IT!

AMÉRICA DEL SUR

COLOMBIA	VENEZUELA	ECUADOR
CIUDAD CAPITAL = CAPITAL CITY		
BOGOTÁ	CARACAS	QUITO
DINERO = MONEY		
PESO	BOLÍVAR	DÓLAR
BANDERA = FLAG		
AMARILLO / AZUL / ROJO	AMARILLO / AZUL / ROJO	AMARILLO / AZUL / ROJO

WHICH ONE IS FALSE? (2 ARE TRUE, SO PUT AN X BY THE FALSE ONE)

Take a class vote. Ask each person to guess if #1, 2 or 3 is the false answer by holding up 1, 2 or 3 fingers. The answers are on p. 118 = ciento dieciocho in the back of this book.

1. Ecuador is near the Equator so there are not four seasons, only two — wet and dry.

2. In Venezuela, the world's highest waterfall is named Salto Ángel = Angel Falls because at 3,212 feet it is near the Angels.

3. Colombia is the only country in South America which touches both the Pacific Ocean and the Caribbean Sea.

ELEMENTARY SPANISH CHATBOOK　　©SPANISH CHAT COMPANY

LECCIÓN 6

🎨 ¡HAZLO! = DO IT!

67
SESENTA Y SIETE

PALO DE LLUVIA = RAINSTICK

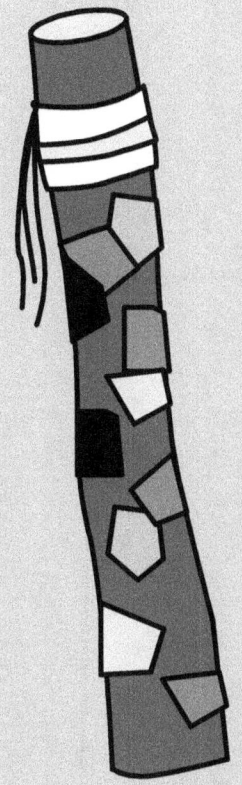

Aztecs believed that shaking a rainstick would bring rain. The original rainsticks were made out of a dried cactus with the cactus spikes nailed back into the hollow tube. Small pebbles were placed inside. Will your rainstick bring rain?

1. Start with an empty paper towel tube or wrapping paper roll.

2. Decorate your rainstick with torn pieces of tissue paper painted onto the outside with glue. This will make a mosaic pattern. Let dry overnight.

3. Cut out two circles from construction paper that are about 1-inch bigger than the end of your tube. Now make 4 half inch cuts from the edge of the circle towards the middle. Fold the circle onto the end of the tube and glue in place.

4. Roll up one square foot of tin foil and stick it into the tube.

5. Place a handful of rice, dried beans or fish rocks inside the tube.

6. Glue the other circle to the empty end of the tube.

7. Shake your rainstick and grab an umbrella just in case.

JOYAS DE ORO = GOLD JEWELRY

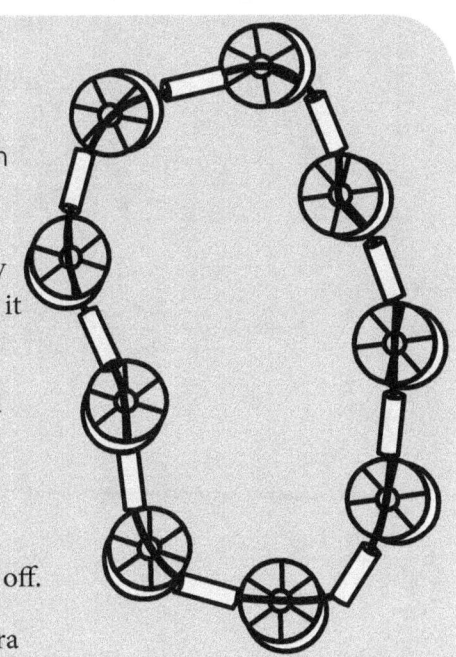

Gold and emeralds can be found in Colombia and other Latin American countries.

1. Spray paint different types of pasta with gold spray paint. You may also use washers, beads or anything with a hole in the middle. Let it dry overnight.

2. Make green esmeralda = emerald pasta by using 3-4 drops of food coloring and 1 Tablespoon of rubbing alcohol in a plastic bag. Shake it to mix and let it dry before using.

3. String the pasta to make necklaces and bracelets or even a mask. Tie a piece of pasta with a knot at one end so the pasta doesn't fall off.

4. A variation is to use small brightly colored beads to make Chaquira Latin American beadwork and jewelry.

ELEMENTARY SPANISH CHATBOOK   ©SPANISH CHAT COMPANY

LECCIÓN 6

¡COCÍNALO! = COOK IT!

Try making the following recipe popular throughout Latin America:

ARROZ CON LECHE = RICE WITH MILK

Remember that an adult will need to help you with anything hot.

ARROZ CON LECHE
(8 cups of pudding)

1. <u>Hierve 4 tazas de agua con canela.</u> = Boil 4 cups of water with a stick of cinnamon.
2. <u>Añade 4 tazas de arroz.</u> = Add 4 cups of rice. Arborio rice is the best for this recipe.
3. <u>Cocínalo.</u> = Cook it according to the rice package directions.
4. <u>Añade 1 lata de leche evaporada.</u> = Add 1 can of evaporated milk.
5. <u>Añade 1 lata de leche condensada.</u> = Add 1 can of sweetened condensed milk.
6. <u>Añade 2 cucharaditas de vainilla.</u> = Add 2 teaspoons of vanilla. Remember to take out the cinnamon stick before serving.
7. <u>Añade canela y mézclalo.</u> = Add cinnamon and mix it. Opcional: Añade pasas, coco o nuez moscada. Optional: Add raisins, coconut or nutmeg.
8. <u>¡Cómelo!</u> = Eat it!
9. <u>¡Mmmm, qué rico!</u> = How tasty!
10. <u>¡Buen provecho!</u> = Bon appetit! Disfruta tu arroz con leche. = Enjoy your rice with milk.

PUERTO RICO: They call it "arroz con dulce" = rice with sweet and they add coconut milk and pistachios.

MEXICO: Sometimes an egg yolk, anise, orange peel, lemon zest or even chocolate are added to variations of their rice pudding.

COLOMBIA: Cream and coffee are sometimes added to the recipe.

¡TERMÍNALO! = FINISH IT!

LECCIÓN 6

69 SESENTA Y NUEVE

UN CALENDARIO PEQUEÑO = A SMALL CALENDAR

Make a mini-calendar. Cut on the dotted edges to make 3 long strips and then fold down the middle. Do NOT cut down the middle. Add birthdays and holidays for your family and friends. Many countries have parades and celebrations for their Independence day = Día de Independencia. Practice saying these dates in Spanish. Add more días festivos = holidays using the guide from pages 114-116 = ciento catorce hasta ciento dieciséis.

Recorta = Cut out along the dashed lines

12 DICIEMBRE
- **16-24 Las Posadas** = The Inns
- **24 Nochebuena** = Christmas Eve
- **25 Navidad** = Christmas
- **31 Nochevieja** = New Year's Eve

1 ENERO
- **1 Año Nuevo** = New Year's
- **1 Día de Liberación** = Liberation Day (Cuba)
- **6 Día de los Reyes Magos** = Day of the Magi Kings

6 JUNIO
- ___ **Día del Padre** = Father's Day

7 JULIO
INDEPENDENCIA DE:
- **4** Puerto Rico
- **5** Venezuela
- **9** Argentina
- **20** Colombia
- **28** Perú

10 OCTUBRE
- **12 Día de la Hispanidad** = Hispanic Day
- **La República de Guinea Ecuatorial** = Equatorial Guinea y **España** = Spain
- **31 Víspera del Día de Todos los Santos** o **Noche de Brujas** = Halloween

3 MARZO

ELEMENTARY SPANISH CHATBOOK © SPANISH CHAT COMPANY

2 FEBRERO

14 Día de San Valentín = Valentine's Day
27 Independencia de La República Dominicana
— Carnaval = Mardi Gras

8 AGOSTO

INDEPENDENCIA DE:
6 Bolivia
10 Ecuador
25 Uruguay

4 ABRIL

— Semana Santa = Holy week
— Pascua = Easter

5 MAYO

1 & 2 Día de los Muertos = Day of the Dead
3 Independencia de Panamá
20 Día del Niño = Children's Day
— Día de Acción de Gracias = Thanksgiving

11 NOVIEMBRE

5 Cinco de Mayo = May 5th
15 Independencia de Paraguay
— Día de la Madre = Mother's Day
— Día del Maestro = Teacher's Day

9 SEPTIEMBRE

INDEPENDENCIA DE:
15 Costa Rica, El Salvador, Guatemala, Honduras, Nicaragua
16 México
18 Chile

LECCIÓN **7** LESSON

HACER = TO DO OR MAKE

¿QUÉ CLIMA HACE HOY? = WHAT IS THE WEATHER DOING TODAY?

- 🌎 Clima = Weather
- 🌎 Chile, Peru & Bolivia
- 🌎 Arte = Art: Arpillera Yarn Art & Moai Statues
- 🌎 Comida = Food: Quinoa
- 🌎 Tarea = Homework: Weather Map

LECCIÓN 7

70 SETENTA

¡REPÍTELO! = REPEAT IT!

Draw a picture for each phrase and repeat them in Spanish. ¡Bravo, muy bien! = Bravo, very good!

¿Qué clima hace hoy? *(KEH Clee-mah Ah-seh Oh/ee?)* What is the weather doing today?	**Hoy hace buen clima.** *(Oh/ee Ah-seh Boo/ehn Clee-mah.)* Today, it is good weather.	**Hace mal clima.** *(Ah-seh Mahl Clee-mah.)* It is bad weather.
Sólo hace un poco de sol. *(SOH-loh Ah-seh Oon Poh-koh Deh Sohl.)* There is only a little bit of sun.	**Hace mucho viento.** *(Ah-seh Moo-cho Vee/ehn-toh.)* There is a lot of wind.	**Hace calor.** *(Ah-seh Kah-lohr.)* It is hot.
Hace frío y llueve. *(Ah-seh FREE/oh Ee You/eh-veh.)* It is cold and it rains.	**¿Qué hago?** **Hago bolas de nieve.** *(Keh Ah-go? Ah-goh Boh-lahs Deh Nee/eh-veh.)* What do I do? I make snowballs.	**¡Ay, ay, ay! ¡Nieva! ¡Cuidado!** *(Ah/ee , ah/ee, ah/ee! Nee/eh-vah! Coo/ee-dah-doh!)* Oh no! It snows! Be careful!

ELEMENTARY SPANISH CHATBOOK ©SPANISH CHAT COMPANY

LECCIÓN 7

71 SETENTA Y UNO

Listen and sing the Weather song. You may want to invent acciones = actions or use sign language for the weather words. Be sure to move your hips for the Cha-Cha-Chas.

CLIMA = WEATHER
Melody: La Cucaracha   Key of E flat

Qué clima, qué clima,
¿Qué clima hace hoy?
¡Cha-cha-cha!
Qué clima, qué clima,
¿Qué clima hace hoy?
¡Cha-cha-cha!

¿Hace buen clima?
¿Hace buen clima?
No. No. No. No. No. No. No.
¡Cha-cha-cha!
¿Hace mal clima?
¿Hace mal clima?
Sí. Sí. Sí. Sí. Sí. Sí. Sí.
¡Cha-cha-cha!

¿Hace sol?
¿Hace sol?
Sólo un poco.
¡Cha-cha-cha!
¿Hace viento?
¿Hace viento?
Sí. Sí. Sí. Mucho. Mucho.
¡Cha-cha-cha!

¿Hace calor?
¿Hace calor?
No. No. No. No. No. No. No.
¡Cha-cha-cha!
¿Hace frío?
¿Hace frío?
Sí. Sí. Sí. Sí. Sí. Sí. Sí.
¡Cha-cha-cha!

¿Llueve? ¿Llueve?
No. No. No. No. No. No. No.
¡Cha-cha-cha!
¿Nieva? ¿Nieva?
Sí. Sí. Sí. Sí. Sí. Sí. Sí.
¡Ay, ay, ay!

¿Qué hago?
¿Qué hago?
Hago bolas de nieve.
¡Cha-cha-cha!
Cuidado. Cuidado,
con las bolas de nieve.
¡Ay, ay, ay!

LECCIÓN 7

72 SETENTA Y DOS

¡¡INTÉNTALO! = TRY IT!

ALREDEDOR DEL MUNDO
A game similar to "Around the World"

IGUAL = SAME

Match the English word with the same Spanish word. Answers are on p. 119 = ciento diecinueve. Now play "Alrededor del Mundo" = "Around the World." The teacher will say the phrase in English using any flashcards from Lessons 1–7. Student #1 will stand behind the chair of Student #2. These two students are competing to be the first person to correctly say the phrase in Spanish. The rest of the group will listen and wait for their turn. The winner is the first of the two students that is able to shout out the phrase. The rest of the group is silent. The winner now advances to the next student on the right and those two try to say the phrase in Spanish. Play continues all the way "around the room/world." The person that defeats the most opponents is the gandador/a = winner.

☐ **1.** Hace frío.   **A** It rains.
                              (ah)

☐ **2.** Hace calor.   **B** It is windy.
                              (beh)

☐ **3.** Hago bolas de nieve. **C** It is bad weather.
                              (seh)

☐ **4.** Hace buen tiempo.   **D** It is hot.
                              (deh)

☐ **5.** Hace viento.   **E** It is sunny.
                              (eh)

☐ **6.** Llueve.   **F** It is cold.
                              (ehf-feh)

☐ **7.** Hace mal tiempo.   **G** It is good weather.
                              (heh)

☐ **8.** Hace sol.   **H** I make snowballs.
                              (ah-cheh)

ELEMENTARY SPANISH CHATBOOK   ©SPANISH CHAT COMPANY

¡LÉELO! = READ IT!

LECCIÓN 7

73
SETENTA Y TRES

Decorate an envelope to hold these game pieces.
Play the "Pares" = "Pairs" game from p. 75 = setenta y cinco.

Recorta = Cut out along the dashed lines

¿Qué clima hace hoy?
(KEH Clee-mah Ah-seh Oh/ee?)

Hace buen clima.
(Ah-seh Boo/ehn Clee-mah.)

Hace mal clima.
(Ah-seh Mahl Clee-mah.)

What is the weather doing today?

It is good weather.

It is bad weather.

Sólo hace un poco de sol.
(SOH-loh Ah-seh Oon Poh-koh Deh Sohl.)

Hace mucho viento.
(Ah-seh Moo-cho Vee/ehn-toh.)

Hace calor.
(Ah-seh Kah-lohr.)

There is only a little bit of sun.

There is a lot of wind.

It is hot.

Hace frío y llueve.
(Ah-seh FREE/oh Ee You/eh-veh.)

¿Qué hago?
Hago bolas de nieve.

¡Ay, ay ay!
¡Nieva! ¡Cuidado!

It is cold and it rains.

What do I do?
I make snowballs.

Oh no!
It snows! Be careful!

ELEMENTARY SPANISH CHATBOOK   ©SPANISH CHAT COMPANY

LECCIÓN 7

 **¡PRACTÍCALO!** = PRACTICE IT!

Play the "Pares" = "Pairs" game described on p. 75 = setenta y cinco.

LECCIÓN 7

PARES
A game similar to "Concentration" or "Matching"

1. To play "Pares" = "Pairs," cut out the matching game cards from p. 73 = setenta y tres. Then make your own game cards using other Spanish vocabulary words and phrases.

2. Glue them onto a piece of construction paper so you are not able to see through.

3. Mix them up and place them face down in rows.

4. Student #1 turns over any two rectangles = rectángulos and reads them aloud while looking for the matching pictures. If they are a match, then Student #1 gets to keep both of the game cards and it is Student #2's turn. If they are not a match, then Student #1 flips both cards back upside down and it is Student #2's turn. Student #1 can say, "Te toca a ti." = "It's your turn."

5. The person with the most matches at the end of the game wins.

TE TOCA A TI. = IT'S YOUR TURN.

¡PARES!

The seasons in South America are opposite from North America. Winter vacation for North America is summer vacation for South America. Children finish school in December and start a new grade in February or March. Countries closer to the Equator may only have two seasons, the wet season and the dry season, instead of the four seasons: Invierno = Winter Primavera = Spring Otoño = Fall and Verano = Summer.

LECCIÓN 7

76 SETENTA Y SEIS

¡MÍRALO! = LOOK AT IT!

AMÉRICA DEL SUR

CHILE	PERÚ	BOLIVIA
CIUDAD CAPITAL = CAPITAL CITY		
SANTIAGO	LIMA	LA PAZ / SUCRE
DINERO = MONEY		
PESO	NUEVO SOL	BOIVIANO
BANDERA = FLAG		
AZUL / BLANCO / ROJO (flag with star)	ROJO / ROJO (flag with crest)	ROJO / AMARILLO / VERDE (flag with crest)

WHICH ONE IS FALSE? (2 ARE TRUE, SO PUT AN X BY THE FALSE ONE)

Take a class vote. Ask each person to guess if #1, 2 or 3 is the false answer by holding up 1, 2 or 3 fingers. The answers are on p. 119 = ciento diecinueve in the back of this book.

○ **1.** The floating islands in Lake Titicaca between Bolivia and Peru are made out of reeds that taste like celery. There is even una escuela flotante = a floating school.

○ **2.** In the Northern Chile Atacama desert, it did not rain for 40 years. Punta Arenas, Chile, is the most Southern city on any continent in the world.

○ **3.** Machu Picchu, Peru, is a city shaped like a jaguar built on top of a mountain. While there you may want to try a bite of cuy = roasted guinea pig at the restaurant.

ELEMENTARY SPANISH CHATBOOK ©SPANISH CHAT COMPANY

¡HAZLO! = DO IT!

LECCIÓN 7

77
SETENTA Y SIETE

ESTATUAS DE MOÁI = MOAI STATUES

Easter Island, Chile, is home to these stone statues that average 13 feet tall and weigh anywhere from 14 to 82 tons.

1. Buy clay or use the Plastalina = Play dough recipe from p. 47 = cuarenta y siete. Each student will need a fist full of clay.

2. Mold it in the form of a Moai statue. The head is usually bigger than the body with a long nose and defined lips.

3. Glue on googly eyes before it dries.

4. Set it out for a few days to dry before you play with it.

ARPILLERAS = YARN ART

South Americans are known for amazing wall hangings depicting familiar scenes from daily life made out of wool and yarn.

1. Gather different colors of yarn and wool.

2. Sketch out your scene onto a piece of paper or poster board. The class can all make the same theme such as a llama or a sunshine.

3. Trace the outline of the sketch with a glue bottle. Now add in your yarn, using different colors and textures.

4. Cotton balls are fun to tear apart and make clouds or llamas.

5. Let dry and then display all of the Arpilleras together.

LLAMAS, VICUÑAS, GUANACOS Y ALPACAS: WHAT IS THE DIFFERENCE?

- Size
- Texture of the fur
- Feel of the wool
- Coloring
- Shape of the ears
- Height

ELEMENTARY SPANISH CHATBOOK   ©SPANISH CHAT COMPANY

LECCIÓN 7

 **78** SETENTA Y OCHO

¡COCÍNALO! = COOK IT!

Try making the following recipe from South America:

SOPA DE QUINUA = QUINOA SOUP

You may want to make a Peruvian meal to accompany this soup. Find recipes for Papa a la Huancaína = Au Gratin type potato dish, Mazamorra morada = Purple corn pudding, Chicha morada = Purple Corn drink or find a bottle of Inca Kola = Yellow Peruvian bubble gum flavored soda.

SOPA DE QUINUA

1. Pica 1 zanahoria, 2 cebollas, 1 tallo de apio y 2 dientes de ajo. = Chop 1 carrot, 2 onions, 1 stalk of celery and 2 cloves of garlic.
2. Saltea todo en 2 cucharadas de aceite de oliva. = Sauté everything in 2 Tablespoons of olive oil. (Be careful to not burn it.)
3. Pon 6 tazas de caldo de pollo y 6 tazas de agua en una olla grande. = Put 6 cups of chicken broth (49 oz.) and 6 cups of water in a big pot.
4. Mézclala con las verduras. = Mix it with the vegetables from step #1 in the pot.
5. Pica 3 papas y ponlas en la olla. = Chop 3 potatoes and put them in the pot.
6. Añade 1 taza de quinua. = Add 1 cup of quinoa.
7. Añade tomillo y albahaca fresco. = Add fresh thyme and basil.
8. Hierve en fuego lento por 20 minutos. = Simmer on low heat for about 20 minutes. The quinoa seeds will split open when they are done.
9. ¡Cómela! = Eat it! ¡Mmmm, qué rico! = How tasty!
10. ¡Buen provecho! Disfruta tu sopa de quinua. = Bon appetit! Enjoy your quinoa soup.

AMÉRICA DEL SUR: South Americans in the Andes mountains have been using "Kinwa" seeds for over 4,000 years.

COMIDA SÚPER: "Super food" Quinoa is full of protein, calcium, iron, fiber, antioxidants and essential amino acids and is even gluten-free.

COLORES: Colors of quinoa are white, red and the traditional black. It can be eaten as a seed, like a grain of rice or puffed like cereal. Quinoa flour is used for cooking South American dishes.

LECCIÓN 7

🏠 ¡TERMÍNALO! = FINISH IT!

¡ADIVÍNALO! = GUESS IT!

Predict and track the weather for six days. Fill out the top row with the day of the week during class and do the row below as homework. Share your work with the class at the beginning of the next lesson. Use the back of this paper to predict and track the weather in South America. Remember that the seasons are opposite from North America.

	Mañana será *(Mah-ñyah-nah Seh-RAH...)* Tomorrow will be... _____ weather	_____ day of the week **será** _____. *(...Seh-RAH...)* weather will be...
¿Qué clima hace hoy? *(KEH Clee-mah Ah-seh Oh/ee?)* What is the weather doing today? _____ weather	**El clima real es** *(Ehl Clee-mah Reh/ahl Ehs...)* The real weather is... _____. weather	**El clima real es** *(Ehl Clee-mah Reh/ahl Ehs...)* The real weather is... _____. weather
_____ day of the week **será** _____. *(...Seh-RAH...)* weather will be...	_____ day of the week **será** _____. *(...Seh-RAH...)* weather will be...	_____ day of the week **será** _____. *(...Seh-RAH...)* weather will be...
El clima real es *(Ehl Clee-mah Reh/ahl Ehs...)* The real weather is... _____ weather	**El clima real es** *(Ehl Clee-mah Reh/ahl Ehs...)* The real weather is... _____ weather	**El clima real es** *(Ehl Clee-mah Reh/ahl Ehs...)* The real weather is... _____ weather

ELEMENTARY SPANISH CHATBOOK ©SPANISH CHAT COMPANY

Predict and track the weather for six days in SOUTH AMERICA. Fill out the top row with the day of the week during class and do the row below as homework. Share your work with the class at the beginning of the next lesson. Since the seasons are opposite from the U.S.A. Feliz Navidad. = Merry Christmas comes in December which is during the hot summertime, so some families celebrate with fireworks and outdoor fiestas = parties and decorate trees with cotton balls for fake snow.

	Mañana será *(Mah-ñyah-nah Seh-RAH...)* Tomorrow will be... _____. weather	_____ day of the week **será** _____. *(...Seh-RAH...)* weather will be...
¿Qué clima hace hoy en América del Sur? *(KEH Clee-mah Ah-seh Oh/ee Ehn Ah-MEHR-ree-kah Dehl Soor?)* What is the weather doing today in South America? _____ weather	**El clima real es** *(Ehl Clee-mah Reh/ahl Ehs...)* The real weather is... _____. weather	**El clima real es** *(Ehl Clee-mah Reh/ahl Ehs...)* The real weather is... _____. weather
_____ day of the week **será** _____. *(...Seh-RAH...)* weather will be...	_____ day of the week **será** _____. *(...Seh-RAH...)* weather will be...	_____ day of the week **será** _____. *(...Seh-RAH...)* weather will be...
El clima real es *(Ehl Clee-mah Reh/ahl Ehs...)* The real weather is... _____. weather	**El clima real es** *(Ehl Clee-mah Reh/ahl Ehs...)* The real weather is... _____. weather	**El clima real es** *(Ehl Clee-mah Reh/ahl Ehs...)* The real weather is... _____. weather

LECCIÓN 8 LESSON

¿QUIERES ALGO? = DO YOU WANT SOMETHING?

- 🌎 Escuela = School
- 🌎 Argentina, Uruguay & Paraguay
- 🌎 Arte = Art: Rastras & Boleadores
- 🌎 Comida = Alfajores
- 🌎 Tarea = Homework: Crazy Classroom

LECCIÓN B

 **¡REPÍTELO!** = REPEAT IT!

Draw a picture to illustrate each word or phrase. Repeat them in Spanish. ¡Sensacional! = Sensational!

¡Ay, ay, ay! Es día de la escuela. No es día de vacaciones. *(Ehs DEE-ah Deh Lah Ehs-coo/eh-lah. Noh Ehs DEE-ah Deh Vah-Kah-see/OH-nehs.)* Oh no! It is a school day. It is not a vacation day.	**¿Quieres algo?** *(Kee/eh-rehs Ahl-goh?)* Do you want something?	**Sí, yo quiero ir al baño.** *(See, Yoh Kee/eh-roh Ee/r Ahl Bah-ñyoh.)* Yes, I want to go to the bathroom.
Escribe con el lápiz y borra las faltas. *(Ehs-cree-beh Kohn Ehl LAH-peez Ee Bohr-rah Lahs Fahl-tahs.)* Write with the pencil and erase the mistakes.	**Recorta el papel con las tijeras y usa un poco de pegamento.** *(Reh-kohr-tah Ehl Pah-pehl Kohn Lahs Tee-heh-rahs Ee Oo-sah Oon Poh-koh Deh Peh-gah-mehn-toh.)* Cut the paper with the scissors and use a little bit of glue.	**Saca el libro y léelo.** *(Sh-kah Ehl Lee-broh Ee LEH/eh-loh.)* Take out the book and read it.
Colorea con los crayones. *(Koh-loh-reh/ah Kohn Lohs Krah-yoh-nehs.)* Color with the crayons.	**Siéntate en la silla a la mesa.** *(See/EHN-tah-teh Ehn Lah See-yah Ah Lah Meh-sah.)* Sit on the chair at the table.	**Levanta la mano para pedir ayuda.** *(Leh-vahn-tah Lah Mah-noh Pah-rah Peh-deer Ah/ee/you-dah.)* Raise your hand to ask for help.

ELEMENTARY SPANISH CHATBOOK ©SPANISH CHAT COMPANY

¡CÁNTALO! = SING IT!

Listen and sing the School song. You may want to use sign language for the classroom words as shown in our Spanish Chatshow videos. Use a backpack or desk full of real objects and hold them up during the correct parts of the song.

ESCUELA = SCHOOL
Melody: Cielito Lindo   Key of E

¡Ay, ay, ay, ay!
Es día de la escuela.
Escribe con el lápiz y
borra las faltas.
Escribe con el lápiz y
borra las faltas.

¡Ay, ay, ay, ay!
Es día de la escuela.
Recorta el papel con las tijeras.
Recorta el papel con las tijeras.

¡Ay, ay, ay, ay!
Es día de la escuela.
Usa un poco de pegamento.
Usa un poco de pegamento.

¡Ay, ay, ay, ay!
Es día de la escuela.
Saca el libro y léelo.
Saca el libro y léelo.

¡Ay, ay, ay, ay!
Es día de la escuela.
Colorea con los crayones.
Colorea con los crayones.

¡Ay, ay, ay, ay!
Es día de la escuela.
Siéntate en la silla a la mesa.
Siéntate en la silla,
a la mesa.

¡Ay, ay, ay, ay!
Es día de la escuela.
Levanta la mano para pedir ayuda.
Levanta la mano,
para pedir ayuda.

¡Ay, ay, ay, ay!
Es día de la escuela.
¿Quieres algo?
¿Quieres algo?
Quiero ir al baño.
Quiero ir al baño.

¡Ay, qué bien!
No es día de la escuela.
Es día de vacaciones.
Es día de vacaciones.
Es día de vacaciones.

LECCIÓN B

¡INTÉNTALO! = TRY IT!

LA MAESTRA / EL MAESTRO
A game similar to "Simon says"

1. To play "La Maestra / El Maestro" = "The Teacher (female/male)," you will need to have students stand up and face the teacher.

2. Review the señas o acciones = signs or actions for each of the school phrases from p. 80 = ochenta.

3. If the teacher states, "Si la maestra dice, 'escribe con el lápiz'" then the students do the action. Each student that does not do the action is then out and can go sit down and practice.

4. If the teacher says, "'colorea' or 'recorta el papel,'" then the students stand quietly with their hands by their sides. If they accidentally do the sign or a motion, then they sit out and practice.

5. Remind them that you will choose one student that has been practicing to get to come back in the game when you get to the "final four." When you get to the final four students, remember to bring back one of these students.

6. Try to trick them by saying, "la maestra dice, 'escribe con el lápiz.'" while you do the action for reading a book. Anyone that does the action for writing with a pencil can stay in, and anyone that copies your book reading action would be out. This is great listening practice.

7. The winner is the final student still in the game.

8. To make the game more difficult use more of the classroom commands found in the back of the book on p. 121 = ciento veintiuno.

SEÑAS O ACCIONES = SIGNS OR ACTIONS

ELEMENTARY SPANISH CHATBOOK   ©SPANISH CHAT COMPANY

¡LÉELO! = READ IT!

LECCIÓN 8

83 OCHENTA Y TRES

Cut out these flashcards and play the "Mochila" = "Backpack" game from p. 85 = ochenta y cinco.

Recorta = Cut out along the dashed lines

¡Ay, ay, ay! Es día de la escuela. No es día de vacaciones.
(Eye, eye, eye, Ehs DEE-ah Deh Lah Ehs-coo/eh-lah. Noh Ehs DEE-ah Deh Vah-Kah-see/OH-nehs.)

LECCIÓN 8

¿Quieres algo?
(Kee/eh-rehs Ahl-goh?)

LECCIÓN 8

Sí, yo quiero ir al baño.
(See, Yoh Kee/eh-roh Ee/r Ahl Bah-ñyoh.)

LECCIÓN 8

Escribe con el lápiz y borra las faltas.
(Ehs-cree-beh Kohn Ehl LAH-peez Ee Bohr-rah Lahs Fahl-tahs.)

LECCIÓN 8

Recorta el papel con las tijeras y usa un poco de pegamento.
(Reh-kohr-tah Ehl Pah-pehl Kohn Lahs Tee-heh-rahs Ee Oo-sah Oon Poh-koh Deh Peh-gah-mehn-toh.)

LECCIÓN 8

Saca el libro y léelo.
(Sh-kah Ehl Lee-broh Ee LEH/eh-loh.)

LECCIÓN 8

Colorea con los crayones.
(Koh-loh-reh/ah Kohn Lohs Krah-yoh-nehs.)

LECCIÓN 8

Siéntate en la silla a la mesa.
(See/EHN-tah-teh Ehn Lah See-yah Ah Lah Meh-sah.)

LECCIÓN 8

Levanta la mano para pedir ayuda.
(Leh-vahn-tah Lah Mah-noh Pah-rah Peh-deer Ah/ee/you-dah.)

LECCIÓN 8

ELEMENTARY SPANISH CHATBOOK   ©SPANISH CHAT COMPANY

LECCIÓN B

¡PRACTÍCALO! = PRACTICE IT!

Play the "Mochila" = "Backpack" game
from 76 = setenta y seis.

Recorta = Cut out along the dashed lines

Yes, I want to go to the bathroom.

Do you want something?

Oh no! It's a school day. It is not a vacation day.

Take out the book and read it.

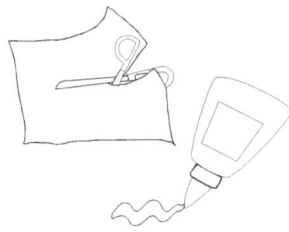
Cut out the paper with the scissors and use a little bit of glue.

Write with the pencil and erase the mistakes.

Raise your hand to ask for help

Sit on the chair at the table.

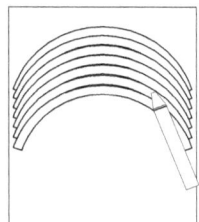
Color with the crayons.

ELEMENTARY SPANISH CHATBOOK ©SPANISH CHAT COMPANY

LECCIÓN B

 ¡JUÉGALO! = PLAY IT!

85
OCHENTA Y CINCO

ESTUDIANTE = STUDENT

MOCHILA
A game similar to "Battleship"

1. To play "Mochila" = "Backpack," you will need a partner. Each partner secretly chooses any three of these items from the list below that you would want in your backpack. You will find some new items on the list and some you may have to make miniatures to fit inside.

2. Draw the items into your backpack and label the items in Spanish without showing your partner. You may want to open a book and stand it up to block your paper.

3. Estudiante = Student #1 says, "¿Quieres el libro en tu mochila?" = "Do you want a book in your backpack?"

4. If Student #2 does not have the book drawn in his/her backpack then Student #2 says, "No, no quiero el libro." = "No, I don't want the book." If they do have the book drawn in the backpack, Student #2 says "Sí, quiero el libro." = "Yes, I do want the book."

5. Now it is Student #2's turn to guess what is in Student #1's backpack.

6. Keep taking turns guessing without peeking in the other person's backpack. The first person to get all three items wins.

el lápiz = the pencil
las tijeras = the scissors
el pegamento = the glue
el libro = the book
los crayones = the crayons
el papel = the paper
la silla = the chair
la mesa = the table
la tarea = the homework
el mapa = the map
la bandera = the flag

ELEMENTARY SPANISH CHATBOOK ©SPANISH CHAT COMPANY

LECCIÓN B

¡MÍRALO! = LOOK AT IT!

AMÉRICA DEL SUR

ARGENTINA | URUGUAY | PARAGUAY

CIUDAD CAPITAL = CAPITAL CITY		
BUENOS AIRES	MONTEVIDEO	ASUNCIÓN

DINERO = MONEY		
PESO	PESO	GUARANÍ

BANDERA = FLAG

Argentina flag: AZUL CLARO / BLANCO / AZUL CLARO

Uruguay flag: BLANCO / AZUL / BLANCO / AZUL / BLANCO / AZUL / BLANCO / AZUL / BLANCO

Paraguay flag: ROJO / BLANCO / AZUL

WHICH ONE IS FALSE? (2 ARE TRUE, SO PUT AN X BY THE FALSE ONE)

Take a class vote. Ask each person to guess if #1, 2 or 3 is the false answer by holding up 1, 2 or 3 fingers. The answers are on p. 119 = ciento diecinueve in the back of this book.

1. Uruguay has never won the Copa Mundial en fútbol = World Cup in soccer.

2. The President of Argentina has his office in the Casa Rosada = Pink House in the Plaza de Mayo = May plaza.

3. Iguazú Waterfalls is twice as wide and even taller than Niagara Falls. It is near the borders of Argentina, Brazil and Paraguay.

ELEMENTARY SPANISH CHATBOOK ©SPANISH CHAT COMPANY

¡HAZLO! = DO IT!

LECCIÓN B

87 OCHENTA Y SIETE

RASTRAS DE GAUCHOS = COWBOY BELTS

Gauchos are the Cowboys from Las Pampas in Argentina and Uruguay. These belts are decorated with plata = silver.

1. Starting at the opening, cut both of the side rectangles out of a paper grocery bag. Leave the bottom of the bag intact.

2. Now open the sack long ways, and cut it into three strips about 4 inches wide and a little more than 3 feet long. Give each student one strip and measure their waist leaving about 6 inches extra.

3. Have students cut one 3-inch oval out of aluminum foil to make a belt buckle. They can write their Spanish name on the buckle with a permanent marker.

4. Students can cut circles out of foil to make silver coins. They can cut other shapes and designs and also decorate the belt with markers.

5. Fit the belt around the student's waist and staple on the top and the bottom of the belt.

BOLEADORAS = BALL ON A STRING

South American Gauchos throw these like lassos to help capture cattle, guanacos and ñandú birds by wrapping them around the animals' legs. Some have two, three or even up to nine balls or weights at the end of the rope.

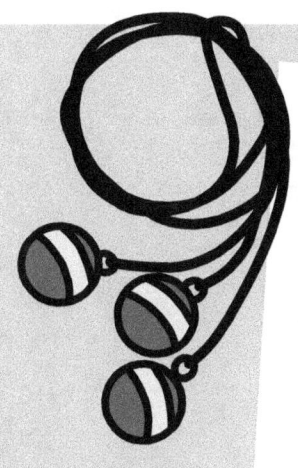

1. Using a permanent marker, have each student decorate two or three plastic Easter eggs or Styrofoam balls.

2. Attach a string inside the egg with a piece of tape, close the egg and then tape it together around the middle.

3. Tie all of the strings together and practice "roping" a chair. Make sure to leave lots of space around each chair or have them practice outside.

TANGO DANCING

1. Play some Argentine Tango music.

2. Walk in a counter clockwise circle around the room.

3. Now walk backwards in the circle. Girls look over their right shoulders and boys look over their left. Lead with your body and then have your feet catch up. Toes are placed on the ground first in Argentina and Uruguay. International Tango style is heel first.

4. Try telling the story with your dramatic movements. Research and add on more Tango steps with partners.

LECCIÓN B

 **¡COCÍNALO!** = COOK IT!

Try making the following recipe from South America:

ALFAJORES = COOKIE WITH CARAMEL FILLING

This is a simplified version to use with kids in a classroom. Research to find more authentic recipes. Before eating this dessert, make a "parrillada" which is a selection of many types of grilled meats. Meat is very plentiful and popular in Argentina, Paraguay and Uruguay. At some all-you-can-eat "parrilla" restaurants, the wait staff walks around carrying skewers and trays with different types of meats. When you nod and smile they add some to your plate.

ALFAJORES

1. Dale 2 galletas a cada estudiante. = Give 2 wafers or shortbread cookies to each student.

2. Pon un poco de dulce de leche sobre una de las galletas. = Put a little bit of "sweetened caramel milk" on top of one cookie.

3. Prueba una con mermelada. = Try one with jam. If you don't have "dulce de leche" use cajeta, caramel ice cream topping, or any flavor of jelly.

4. Pon una galleta arriba de la otra galleta. = Put one cookie on top of the other cookie.

5. Calienta el chocolate. = Heat up the chocolate. Use any types of chocolate, sometimes they make "blanco y negro" which is half white chocolate and half dark chocolate.

6. Ponla en el chocolate. = Put it in the chocolate.

7. ¡Cómela! = Eat it!

8. ¡Mmmm, qué rico! = How tasty!

9. ¡Buen provecho! = Bon appetit,

10. Disfruta tus alfajores. = Enjoy your cookies.

ARGENTINA/URUGUAY: Alfajores are coated in dark or white chocolate, powdered sugar, or a "nieve" = snow coating of egg whites and sugar.

ESPAÑA: In Spain, Alfajores are sold mostly during the Christmas season and can be made with flour, honey, almonds, hazelnuts and spices such as cinnamon.

ALAJÚ: The Arabic version with almond, honey and figs wrapped in a wafer and is still made today in Cuenca, Spain. Many years ago, the ingredients had to be adapted when the recipe was brought to South America.

LECCIÓN 8

🏠 **¡TERMÍNALO!** = FINISH IT!

EL SALÓN RARO = THE STRANGE CLASSROOM

Use the list of school words from the "Mochila" = "Backpack" game on p. 85 = ochenta y cinco. Draw a classroom where you hide the different objects in strange places or a crazy classroom where someone will try to guess the 10 things wrong with your picture. Use the back of this paper to make a list of the 10 correct answers.

ELEMENTARY SPANISH CHATBOOK © SPANISH CHAT COMPANY

LAS RESPUESTAS = THE ANSWERS

Here is the list of the 10 different objects hidden in strange places or the 10 things wrong with the drawing on p. 89 = ochenta y nueve.

1. _____

2. _____

3. _____

4. _____

5. _____

6. _____

7. _____

8. _____

9. _____

10. _____

LECCIÓN 9 LESSON

VER = TO SEE

¿CUÁLES COLORES VES AQUÍ? = WHAT COLORS DO YOU SEE HERE?

- 🌎 Colores = Colors
- 🌎 Ropa = Clothing
- 🌎 Puerto Rico, Cuba & Dominican Republic
- 🌎 Arte = Art: Masks & Favorite Holidays
- 🌎 Comida = Food: Cuban Sandwich
- 🌎 Tarea = Homework: Clothing Store & Counting Clothes In Your Room

LECCIÓN 9

¡REPÍTELO! = REPEAT IT!

Draw a picture to illustrate each phrase. Repeating them in Spanish. ¡Buen Trabajo! = Good work!

¿Cuáles colores ves aquí? *(Kwah-lehs Koh-loh-rehs Vehs Ah-KEE?)* Which colors do you see here?	**Yo veo la camisa roja.** *(Yoh Veh-oh Lah Kah-mee-sah Roh-hah.)* I see the red shirt.	**los pantalones azules** *(Lohs Pahn-tah-loh-nehs Ah-zoo-lehs)* the blue pants
el traje de baño amarillo y verde *(Ehl Trah-heh Deh Bah-ñyoh Ah-mah-ree-yoh Ee Vehr-deh.)* the yellow and green swimsuit	**la chaqueta rosa, morada y violeta** *(Lah Chah-keh-tah Roh-sah, Moh-rah-dah Ee Vee-oh-leh-tah.)* the pink, purple and violet jacket	**la falda anaranjada** *(Lah Fahl-dah Ah-nah-rahn-hah-dah)* the orange skirt
los zapatos negros *(Lohs Zah-pah-tohs Neh-grohs)* the black shoes	**la gorra gris** *(Lah Gohr-rah Grees)* the gray cap	**Lava los calcetines blancos y cafés ahora.** *(Lah-vah Lohs Kahl-seh-tee-nehs Blahn-kohs Ee Kah-FEHS Ah-oh-rah.)* Wash the white and brown socks now.

ELEMENTARY SPANISH CHATBOOK   ©SPANISH CHAT COMPANY

 = SING IT!

LECCIÓN 9

91
NOVENTA Y UNO

Listen and sing the "Clothing of Many Colors" song. Students may stand up and sit down during the song if they are wearing that particular color. Another idea is to give students flyswatters or pointers and have them point to or touch the color around the room as they hear it. Remind them not to actually touch other students with the pointers.

ROPA DE MUCHOS COLORES = CLOTHING OF MANY COLORS
Melody: Row, Row, Row Your Boat   Key of B flat

Rojo, rojo, ro-jo-jo,
Azul, azul, azul,
Amarillo, amarillo,
Verde, verde, verde.

Mor-mor-morado,
Violeta, violeta,
Anaranjado, anaranjado,
Rosa, rosa, rosa.

Negro, negro, ne-gro-gro,
Café, café, café,
Blanco, blanco, blanco, blanco,
Gris, gris, gris.

¿Cuáles colores ves aquí?
¿Cuáles colores ves?
Veo la camisa roja,
la camisa roja.

Veo los pantalones azules,
los pantalones azules.
Veo la gorra gris,
la gorra gris.

Veo el traje de baño,
amarillo y verde,
el traje de baño,
amarillo y verde.

Veo la chaqueta rosa,
morada y violeta,
la chaqueta rosa,
morada y violeta.

Veo la falda anaranjada,
la falda anaranjada.
Veo los zapatos negros,
los zapatos negros.

Veo los calcetines blancos,
los calcetines blancos.
¡Ay, ay, ay!
¡Calcetines cafés,
los calcetines cafés!

¡Lávalos ahora!
¡Lávalos ahora!

ELEMENTARY SPANISH CHATBOOK   ©SPANISH CHAT COMPANY

LECCIÓN 9

¡INTÉNTALO! = TRY IT!

DESFILE DE MODA
A game similar to a "Fashion Show"

1. To play "Desfile de Moda" = "Fashion Show," find a microfono = microphone or use a botella de agua = water bottle.

2. Find a partner. Look at what your partner is wearing and fill in the blanks in the gray box to match your partner's outfit. Your partner will be the girl "la modela" or boy "el modelo" = model while you are the la presentadora o el presentador = the female or male presenter and then you will switch places.

3. La modelo o el modelo = the female or male model will walk around the designated runway area. It is fun to let the students use their imagination and exaggerate their fashion walk. If you put on Latin music, they can dance down the aisle. Quieter students may want to find an amiga o amigo = female or male friend to walk with to make it easier.

4. While the modelo is walking the runway another student will be la presentadora o el presentador = the female or male presenter. Using a micrófono = microphone, this person will announce, "Veo los pantalones azules y la camisa roja con los calcetines blancos y los zapatos cafés." = "I see the blue pants and the red shirt with the white socks and the brown shoes." Each presenter would change the colors to fit what the model is wearing. For the younger students, the adult will be the announcer allowing them to fill in the colors as you talk. You may say, "Veo los pantalones...y la camisa...."

MODELA O MODELO = MODEL

VEO...

1. los pantalones
   _____

2. la camisa
   _____

3. los calcetines
   _____

4. los zapatos
   _____

5. otros = others
   _____

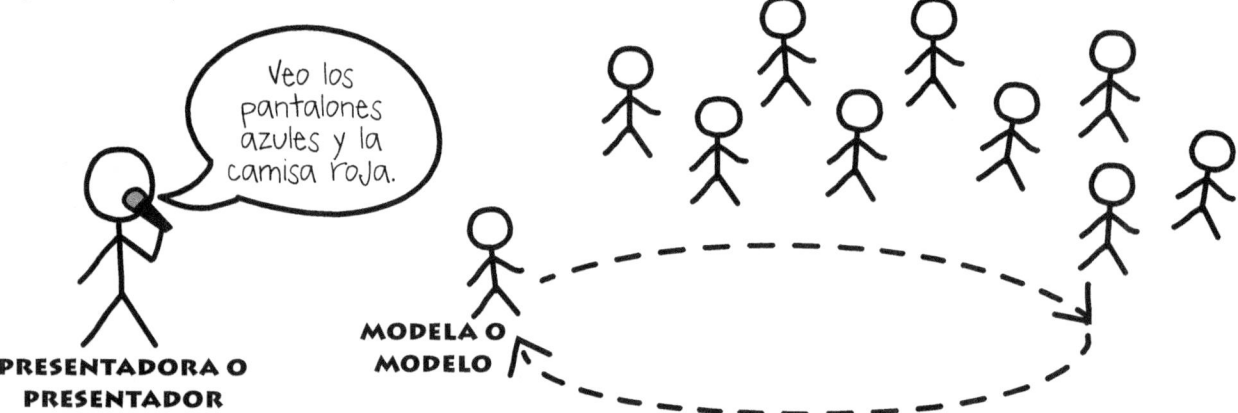

ELEMENTARY SPANISH CHATBOOK   ©SPANISH CHAT COMPANY

LECCIÓN 9

¡LÉELO! = READ IT!

93 NOVENTA Y TRES

Cut out and staple the book in the top left corner. Interview someone by reading the book to that person in Spanish and marking what colors they are wearing. *Cut along the dashed lines*

Recorta = Cut out along the dashed lines

Hola. ¿Cómo estás?
(Oh-lah. KOH-moh Ehs-TAHS?)
Hello. How are you?

Ask your listener what colors of clothing they are wearing. Keep track by using tally marks. In South America, some people write tally marks in a square. Start by drawing a line down and continue following the example.

1

¿Cómo te llamas?
(KOH-moh Teh Yah-mahs?)
What is your name?

Me llamo...
(Meh Yah-moh...)
My name is...
(Sign your name on the line below.)

_____

_____

_____

_____

_____

3

Veo el traje de baño...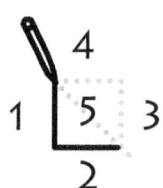
(Veh-oh Ehl Trah-heh Deh Bah-ñyoh...)
I see the swimsuit...

AMARILLO

VERDE   OTRO

Veo la falda...
(Veh-oh Lah Fahl-dah...)
I see the skirt...

ANARANJADA

AZUL   OTRA

5

Veo los calcetines...
(Veh-oh Lohs Kahl-seh-tee-nehs...)
I see the socks...

CAFÉS   OTROS

BLANCOS

Veo los zapatos...
(Veh-oh Lohs Zah-pah-tohs...)
I see the shoes..

BLANCOS

NEGROS   OTROS

7

ELEMENTARY SPANISH CHATBOOK   ©SPANISH CHAT COMPANY

LECCIÓN 9

¡PRACTÍCALO! = PRACTICE IT!

Cut out this book and staple it. Have a contest to see who can read it to the most people this week.

Recorta = Cut out along the dashed lines

Veo los pantalones...
(Veh-oh Lohs Pahn-tah-loh-nehs...)
I see the pants...

CAFÉS   AZULES

OTROS

Veo los pantalones cortos...
(Veh-oh Lohs Pahn-tah-loh-nehs Kohr-tohs...)
I see the shorts...

CAFÉS   NEGROS

OTROS

Veo la camisa...
(Veh-oh Lah Kah-mee-sah...)
I see the shirt...

ROJA   AZUL

OTRA

4

Estoy bien.
(Ehs-toy Bee/ehn.)
I am well.

SÍ   NO

Estoy cansada o cansado.
(Ehs-toy Kahn-sah-dah Oh Kahn-sah-doh.)
I am tired. (female or male)

SÍ   NO

Estoy enferma o enfermo.
(Ehs-toy Ehn-fehr-mah Oh Ehn-fehr-moh.)
I am sick. (female or male)

SÍ   NO

2

Gracias.
(Grah-see/ahs.)
Thank you.

Hasta luego.
(Ahs-tah Loo/eh-goh.)
See you later.

8

Veo la chaqueta...
(Veh-oh Lah Chah-keh-tah...)
I see the jacket...

MORADA

ROSA   OTRA

Veo la gorra...
(Veh-oh Lah Gohr-rah...)
I see the cap...

VIOLETA

GRIS   OTRA

6

ELEMENTARY SPANISH CHATBOOK   ©SPANISH CHAT COMPANY

 ¡JUÉGALO! = PLAY IT!

LECCIÓN 9

95
NOVENTA Y CINCO

ESTILO DE ROPA
A game called "Clothing Style"

 = 5

1. To play "Estilo De Ropa" = "Clothing Style," use the outline of the person below.

2. Roll the dice 12 times. After each roll, you will fill in the 12 lines with the color words that match the roll of your dice. For example; 4 + 1 = 5 which is the color anaranjado = orange.

3. Now color the crazy outfits onto the outline and add a cara = face to your person.

4. Show your Estilo de Ropa to a partner and read the list of clothing and colors in Spanish.

COLORES
2. rojo
3. azul
4. amarillo
5. verde
6. anaranjado
7. blanco
8. violeta
9. rosa
10. negro
11. café
12. gris

VEO...

1. los pantalones:

   _____ y _____

2. la camisa:

   _____ y _____

3. los calcetines:

   _____ y _____

4. los zapatos:

   _____ y _____

5. la gorra:

   _____ y _____

6. la chaqueta:

   _____ y _____

ELEMENTARY SPANISH CHATBOOK   ©SPANISH CHAT COMPANY

LECCIÓN 9

¡MÍRALO! = LOOK AT IT!

PUERTO RICO	CUBA	LA REPÚBLICA DOMINICANA
CIUDAD CAPITAL = CAPITAL CITY		
SAN JUAN	HABANA	SANTO DOMINGO
DINERO = MONEY		
DÓLAR	PESO	PESO
BANDERA = FLAG		
AZUL, BLANCO, ROJO, BLANCO, ROJO (with white star)	ROJO, BLANCO, AZUL, BLANCO, AZUL (with white star)	AZUL, ROJO, BLANCO, ROJO, AZUL

WHICH ONE IS FALSE? (2 ARE TRUE, SO PUT AN X BY THE FALSE ONE)

Take a class vote. Ask each person to guess if #1, 2 or 3 is the false answer by holding up 1, 2 or 3 fingers. The answers are on p. 119 = ciento diecinueve in the back of this book.

1. The island of Cuba is shaped like a cocodrilo = crocodile.

2. The coquí frog in Puerto Rico sings/croaks all day long and is quiet all night.

3. If you ordered "la bandera" in a Dominican Republic restaurant you would get arroz, frijoles y carne = rice, beans and some type of meat.

 **¡HAZLO!** = DO IT!

LECCIÓN 9

97
NOVENTA Y SIETE

1. Color the Máscara = Mask.

2. Decorate it with multicolored feathers and let the glue dry. You may also want to decorate with glitter.

3. Cut out both the mask and the center eye holes.

4. Punch holes where the X is on each side.

5. Cut a pipe cleaner in half and put each half through one of the holes you just punched.

6. Bend the pipe cleaners around your orejas = ears like eyeglasses.

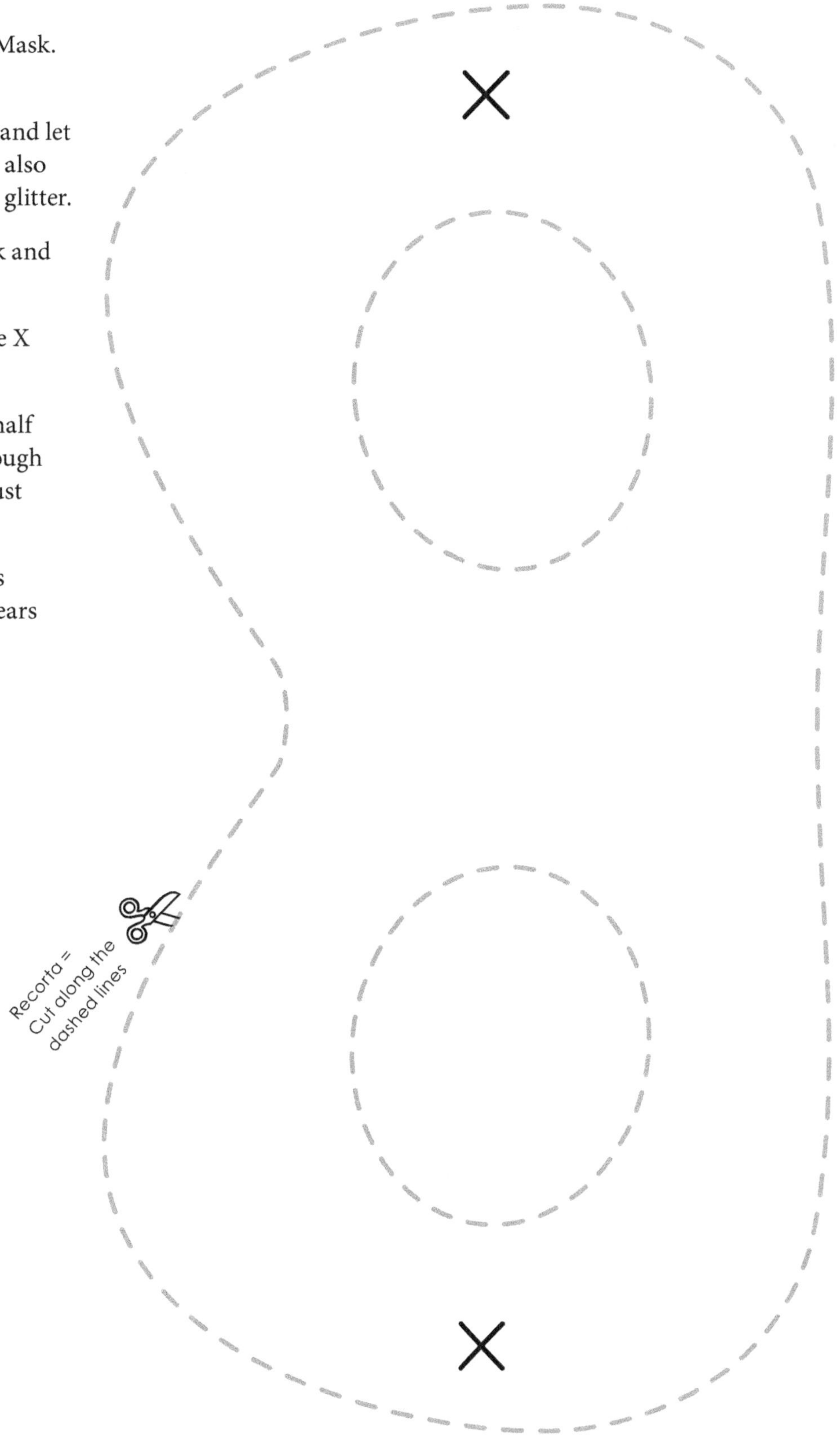

Recorta = Cut along the dashed lines

DÍAS FESTIVOS = HOLIDAYS

Arte = Art continued: Draw a picture including costumes and customs from various Latin American holidays. Use the holiday guide from the back of the book on pages 114-116 = ciento catorce hasta ciento dieciséis.

LECCIÓN 9

¡COCÍNALO! = COOK IT!

Try making the following recipe popular in Florida, New York, Puerto Rico and other communities that have Cuban immigrants.

SÁNDWICH CUBANO / MEDIANOCHE / MIXTO = CUBAN SANDWICH / MIDNIGHT / MIXED

Remember that an adult will need to help you with anything hot.

SÁNDWICH CUBANO / MEDIANOCHE / MIXTO

1. **Compra pan.** = Buy bread. If you are unable to find cuban bread, then use a loaf of French bread, a baguette or even plain white sandwich bread.

2. **Córtalo.** = Cut it lengthwise.

3. **Pon la mostaza.** = Put on the mustard. You may use mayonnaise.

4. **Añade el jamón y el lomo asado.** = Add the ham and roasted pork. Add salami if you want.

5. **Ponle queso suizo.** = Put on swiss cheese.

6. **Añade los pepinos.** = Add the pickles. You may also want to add lettuce and tomato.

7. **Pon un poco de mantequilla.** = Put on a little bit of butter or olive oil onto the crust side of the bread.

8. **Plánchalo.** = "Iron it." Use a sandwich press or panini maker. If you don't have one, then put a heavy skillet on top of the sandwiches before grilling or baking in the oven. This will press them flat. Bake them in the oven at 350 degrees until the cheese is melted.

9. **¡Cómelo!** = Eat it! ¡Mmmm, qué rico! = How tasty!

10. **¡Buen provecho!** = Bon appetit! Disfruta tu sándwich cubano = Enjoy your cuban sandwich.

MEDIANOCHE: Midnight is the name of the sandwich served in Cuba and Puerto Rico on a soft yellow egg bread. It is sweet and similar to the Jewish bread called Challah.

MEXICO: Order a "Torta Cubano" which is a sandwich made with different meats.

TOSTONES/PATACONES: Fry some green plantains, smash them and refry them to make a side dish to go with your sandwich.

PLATANOS MADUROS FRITOS: Fry a ripe yellow banana and it will caramelize, making it another option to accompany your Medianoche.

¡TERMÍNALO! = FINISH IT!

MI TIENDA DE ROPA = MY CLOTHING STORE

Draw your own tienda de ropa = clothing store with prices. "Los zapatos cuestan...." = "The shoes cost...." To practice colors, play "Yo Veo" = "I Spy." One person secretly spies something and says, "Yo veo el color café." = "I see the color brown." The other people have to guess what it is. Another homework project is described on the next page.

EN MI CUARTO = IN MY ROOM

Count clothes in your closets and drawers and bring back a list. For example, "Yo veo cinco camisas negras en mi cuarto." = "I see five black shirts in my room." Use the list below to get you started.

YO VEO...

1. _____ pantalones:
   #

_____ y _____
   color   color

2. _____ camisas:
   #

_____ y _____
   color   color

3. _____ calcetines:
   #

_____ y _____
   color   color

4. _____ zapatos:
   #

_____ y _____
   color   color

5. _____ gorras:
   #

_____ y _____
   color   color

6. _____ chaquetas:
   #

_____ y _____
   color   color

LESSON **10** LECCIÓN

IR = TO GO
COMER = TO EAT

¿QUÉ VAS A COMER? = WHAT ARE YOU GOING TO EAT?

- 🌎 Comidas y Bebidas = Foods & Drinks

- 🌎 La República de Guinea Ecuatorial = Equatorial Guinea

- 🌎 Arte = Art: Cuban Piñata & Maracas

- 🌎 Comida = Food: Tropical Fruit Salad

- 🌎 Tarea = Homework: Ten Ways To Practice Spanish & Ten Project Ideas

- 🌎 Certificado = Certificate

LECCIÓN 10

¡REPÍTELO! = REPEAT IT!

Draw a picture to illustrate each word or phrase. Repeating them in Spanish. ¡Maravilloso! = Marvelous!

¿Qué vas a comer? *(Keh Vahs Ah Koh-mehr?)* What are you going to eat?	Yo voy a comer yogur con frutas. *(Yoh Voh/ee Ah Koh-mehr Yoh-goor Kohn Froo-tahs.)* I am going to eat yogurt with fruit.	cereal con leche para el desayuno *(Seh-reh/ahl Kohn Leh-che Pah-rah Ehl Deh-sah-you-noh)* cereal with milk for breakfast
ensalada de verduras para el almuerzo *(Ehn-sah-lah-dah Deh Vehr-doo-rahs Pah-rah Ehl Ahl-moo/ehr-zoh)* vegetable salad for lunch	arroz con pollo para la cena *(Ahr-rohz Kohn Poh-yoh Pah-rah Lah Seh-nah)* rice with chicken for dinner	helado de fresa para el postre *(Eh-lah-doh Deh Freh-sah Pah-rah Ehl Pohs-treh)* strawberry ice cream for the dessert
carne con papas para la fiesta *(Kahr-neh Kohn Pah-pahs Pah-rah Lah Fee/ehs-tah)* meat with potatoes for the party	Estoy llena. Estoy lleno. *(Ehs-toh/ee Yeh-nah.)* *(Ehs-toh/ee Oh Yeh-noh.)* I am full. (girl/boy)	Yo voy a tomar una siesta. *(Yoh Voh/ee Ah Toh-mahr Oo-nah See/ehs-tah.)* I am going to take a nap.

♪ ¡CÁNTALO! = SING IT!

LECCIÓN 10

Listen and sing along with this "Food" song. Act it out using fake or real food. You may want to use visuals of the foods and have different students stand up with the signs during the song.

COMIDA = FOOD
Melody: Los Pollitos   Key of B flat

Voy a comer...
Voy a comer...
yogur con frutas,
yogur con frutas,
carne con papas,
carne con papas,
para la fiesta,
para la fiesta.

cereal con leche,
cereal con leche,
para el desayuno,
para el desayuno,

¿Qué vas a comer?
¿Qué vas a comer?
No voy a comer.
No voy a comer.

ensalada de verduras,
ensalada de verduras,
para el almuerzo,
para el almuerzo,

Voy a tomar
una siesta.
Voy a tomar
una siesta.

arroz con pollo,
arroz con pollo,
para la cena,
para la cena,

👧 Estoy llena.

👦 Estoy lleno.

Buenas noches.
Buenas noches.

helado de fresa,
helado de fresa,
para el postre,
para el postre,

LECCIÓN 10

¡INTÉNTALO! = TRY IT!

PÁSALO
Play a game similar to "Pass the Egg"

1. To play "Pásalo" = "Pass It," you will need two sets of fake food or two visuals of each food mentioned on p. 100 = cien. Draw the visuals or cut food pictures out of ads or magazines. You may want to laminate these.

2. Form two equal lines of students. If you have one extra student, have the last person in that line stand up and be the juez = judge each time.

3. Put the foods/visuals at the front of each line and a grocery bag at the end of each line.

4. Maestra/maestro = The teacher (female/male) will say "Voy a comer yogur. Pásalo." The student at the front of the line will then find the empty yogurt cup or the yogurt visual and pass it down the line as quickly as possible. The first team to put the item in the grocery bag gets two points. The second team gets one point if it is the correct item.

5. Have the students in each team chant the name of the item as they pass it down the line, such as "yogur, yogur...."

6. Now have the last person in each line come to the front of the line and everyone move back. The judge will come to the front and the last person on that team will be the new judge.

7. The team with the most points wins.

LECCIÓN 10

 ¡LÉELO! = READ IT!

103
CIENTO TRES

Decorate an envelope to hold these flashcards. Cut them out and play "Verdad O Falso" game from p. 105 = ciento cinco.

Recorta = Cut out along the dashed lines

¿Qué vas a comer?
(Keh Vahs Ah Koh-mehr?)

LECCIÓN 10

Voy a comer yogur con frutas.
(Voh/ee Ah Koh-mehr Yoh-goor Kohn Froo-tahs.)

LECCIÓN 10

---

cereal con leche para el desayuno
(Seh-reh/ahl Kohn Leh-che Pah-rah Ehl Deh-sah-you-noh)

LECCIÓN 10

---

ensalada con verduras para el almuerzo
(Ehn-sah-lah-dah Kohn Vehr-doo-rahs Pah-rah Ehl Ahl-moo/ehr-zoh)

LECCIÓN 10

---

arroz con pollo para la cena
(Ahr-rohz Kohn Poh-yoh Pah-rah Lah Seh-nah)

LECCIÓN 10

---

helado de fresa para el postre
(Eh-lah-doh Deh Freh-sah Pah-rah Ehl Pohs-treh)

LECCIÓN 10

---

carne con papas para la fiesta
(Kahr-neh Kohn Pah-pahs Pah-rah Lah Fee/ehs-tah)

LECCIÓN 10

 **Estoy llena.**
Estoy lleno.
(Ehs-toh/ee Yeh-nah. Ehs-toh/ee Yeh-noh.)

LECCIÓN 10

Yo voy a tomar una siesta.
(Yoh Voh/ee Ah Toh-mahr Oo-nah See/ehs-tah.)

LECCIÓN 10

ELEMENTARY SPANISH CHATBOOK ©SPANISH CHAT COMPANY

LECCIÓN 10

 ¡PRACTÍCALO! = PRACTICE IT!

Play the game on p. 105 = ciento cinco using these flashcards.

Recorta = Cut out along the dashed lines

cereal with milk for breakfast

I am going to eat yogurt with fruit.

What are you going to eat?

strawberry ice cream for the dessert

rice with chicken for the dinner

vegetable salad for the lunch

I am going to take a nap.

I am full. (girl)
I am full. (boy)

beef with potatoes for the party

LECCIÓN 10

 ¡JUÉGALO! = PLAY IT!

VERDAD O FALSO
A game similar to "Two Truths and a Lie"

DEDOS = FINGERS

1. To play "Verdad O Falso" = "Truth Or Lie," choose any flashcards from Lessons 1-9.

2. Write down two sentences that are true and one sentence that is false. For example,
    #1 "No estoy cansada." = I am not tired.
    #2 "Voy a comer bistec para el desayuno." = I am going to eat steak for breakfast.
    #3 "Me gusta nadar." = I like to swim.

3. Read your sentences to a partner or in front of the entire class.

4. Ask each person to guess if #1, 2 or 3 is the false answer by holding up 1, 2 or 3 dedos = fingers.

5. Reveal the correct answer and switch partners or let the next person share theirs with the class. Mine is #2 because I am not going to eat steak for breakfast.

UNA MENTIRA = A LIE

1. _____

2. _____

3. _____

School schedules and eating times are different in Latin America. Due to overcrowding and lack of money, some students only go to school in the morning and other students only go to school in the afternoons. Although elementary school is usually mandatory, some students still can't afford the books and uniforms and are unable to go to more than a few years of classes. In Spain, elementary students eat desayuno = breakfast and go to school from 9-12 then have a three hour almuerzo y recreo = lunch and recess. Around 2 pm is the biggest meal of the day and many stores in Spain still close for this siesta time. Children will have school again from 3-5 in the tarde= afternoon and then have a merienda = snack. Cena = supper is a sandwich or small meal around 8 p.m.

LECCIÓN 10

¡MÍRALO! = LOOK AT IT!

LA REPÚBLICA DE GUINEA ECUATORIAL =
EQUATORIAL GUINEA

CIUDAD CAPITAL = CAPITAL CITY	**DINERO** = MONEY
MALABO	**CENTRAL AFRICAN CFA FRANC**

BANDERA = FLAG

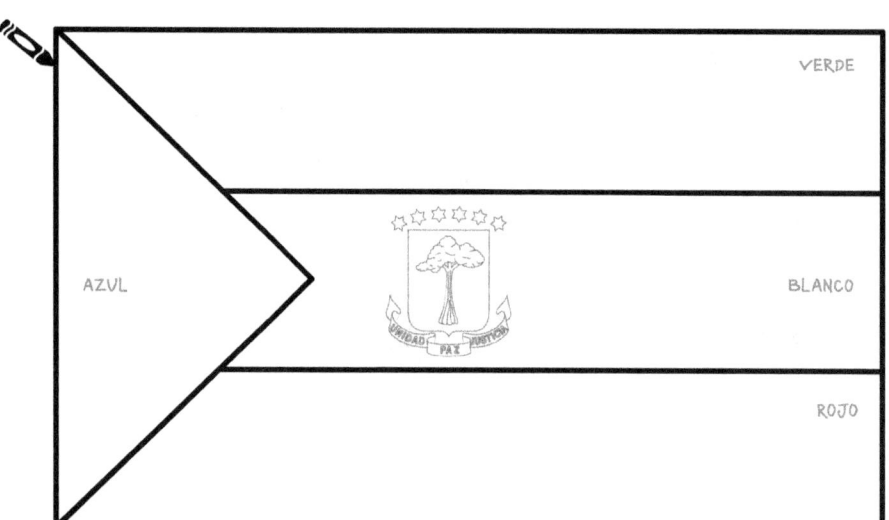

WHICH ONE IS FALSE? (2 ARE TRUE, SO PUT AN X BY THE FALSE ONE)

Take a class vote. Ask each person to guess if #1, 2 or 3 is the false answer by holding up 1, 2 or 3 fingers. The answers are on p. 119 = ciento diecinueve in the back of this book.

1. La República de Guinea Ecuatorial = Equatorial Guinea is one of the smallest countries in Africa located just across the ocean from Spain.

2. Río Muni has a dry season from junio hasta agosto = June until August while Bioko has a wet season. Río Muni has a wet, rainy season from diciembre hasta febrero = December until February while Bioko has a dry season.

3. Equatoguinean Swimmers "Eric the Eel" and "Paula the Crawler" had some of the slowest times ever recorded during the Olympics. It was Eric's first time in a pool since he always practiced in a lake.

¡HAZLO! = DO IT!

PIÑATA CUBANO = CUBAN PIÑATA

Piñatas are found at celebrations and fiestas in many Spanish-speaking countries. Cuban piñatas are broken by having each child pull a string instead of hitting it with a stick.

1. Decorate a paper bag upside down so the hole is at the bottom. Make it look like an animal with colored paper, fringe, feathers and glue.

2. Fill the bag with stickers, candies, bookmarks, pencils, mini-notepads or other prizes. Write positive Spanish phrases on small pieces of paper using the list in the back of the book on p. 120 = ciento veinte.

3. Punch holes and tie strings to the top edge of the bag.

4. Staple the bag shut.

5. When you are ready to break your Cuban piñata, give one each student one string and say, "Uno, dos, tres, ¡Vámonos!" = "1, 2, 3, let's go!"

MARACAS = MARACAS

A Latin American instrument made out of a dried gourd or coconut shell, leather, wood or plastic. Maracas are usually filled with dried beans or seeds.

1. "Reuse" a plastic water bottle or any container with a lid. Make sure it is clean and dry inside.

2. Decorate your maraca with colored paper and markers.

3. Glue the tops of the 1-inch strips of tissue paper to make streamers.

4. Fill with dried pasta and glue the lid shut.

5. Invite the parents to come at the end of class. Do the Alphabet Raspa dance from p. 11 = once and any other songs. Shake your maraca during a parade around the room or outside. Break your piñata together. Es una fiesta. = It's a party.

LECCIÓN 10

 **¡COCÍNALO!** = COOK IT!

Try making the following recipe from Spain:

ENSALADA DE FRUTAS TROPICALES = TROPICAL FRUIT SALAD

This dish will include fruits from the rainforest that you have never tried. Try buying one new fruit or vegetable each week at the store and find a recipe that uses it. You may want to find other recipes from Latin America to try. Keep trying. = Sigue intentando.

ENSALADA DE FRUTAS TROPICALES

1. Corta y pela una papaya. = Cut and peel a papaya.
2. Corta y pela un mango y un kiwi. = Cut and peel a mango and a kiwi.
3. Corta y pela una piña. = Cut and peel a pineapple.
4. Añade otras frutas como guayaba, carambola o bananas. = Add other fruits like guava, star fruit or bananas. Any type of berries, oranges, apples and grapes would also taste great. Be creative and try any other tropical fruits you are able to find.
5. Hornea una taza de coco. = Bake one cup of shredded coconut on a cookie sheet in a 350 degree oven for five minutes or until lightly toasted.
6. Pon miel y crema batida. = Put on honey and whipped cream. You may also use yogurt.
7. ¡Cómela! = Eat it!
8. ¡Mmmm, qué rico! = How tasty!
9. ¡Buen provecho! = Bon appetit!
10. Disfruta tu ensalada de frutas tropicales. = Enjoy your tropical fruit salad.

FRESCO DE FRUTAS: In Costa Rica, they pour a sweet strawberry syrup or a fruity carbonated soda on top of the fruits.

BATIDO/LICUADO: Blend tropical fruits together with milk and ice to make a milkshake.

GELATINA: Try to find gelatin mixes in different flavors such as mango or pineapple. Try using pudding mixes such as a box of flan (custard) and temblique, a coconut gelatin dessert.

LECCIÓN 10

 ¡TERMÍNALO! = FINISH IT!

UN POCO MÁS = A LITTLE MORE

Now that you have made it to the final lesson of the book, the question is, "How do you continue the learning?" The most important thing is to practice, practice, practice. Here are ten ways to continue practicing and learning the Spanish language:

1. **Estudia** = Study: Keep your book and flashcards handy and use them often. Type up lists of the phrases and laminate them to post on your refrigerator or in your room. Practice games with your flashcards. Try one of the project ideas listed on the p. 110 = ciento diez. Take the examen on p. 117 = ciento diecisiete.

2. **Almuerzo** = Lunch: Organize a lunch led by a Spanish speaker. Speak in Spanish about your interests, current events, or what is happening in your life. Meet the first Friday of each month to chat in Spanish Have a family lunch or dinner where everyone is required to speak Spanish.

3. **Habla** = Talk: Create opportunities for speaking Spanish. Ask native speakers questions in Spanish and learn the appropriate response. Learn a new phrase each and every day. Use the examen from p. 117 = ciento diecisiete to help you ask and answer questions.

4. **Clases** = Classes: Find more Spanish lessons or create a class with your friends and family. Sign up for an online class or check out Spanish books and materials from your local library.

5. **Día Especial** = Special Day: Pick a day and incorporate Spanish as much as possible. Plan a specific day to practice your phrases. Greet others and ask questions in Spanish

6. **Amigos** = Friends: Look for a native speaker who would like to help you speak Spanish and practice together often. With adult help, try to connect and pen pal with someone that actually lives in Latin America.

7. **La Vida Latina** = The Latin Life: Listen to Spanish music and learn some popular songs. Listen to a Spanish radio station in the car, or watch a Spanish TV channel. With an adult's help, find and read newspapers from all over Latin America.

8. **Cultura** = Culture: There is a lot of diversity in the Spanish-speaking world. Find Hispanic cultural activities nearby. Visit travel Web sites. Take a family vacation to spend a week at a language school in Latin America or with a church-sponsored mission trip.

9. **Búsqueda** = Scavenger hunt: Use the Supermercado = Supermarket scavenger hunt/field trip from p. 112 = ciento doce. Buy five new items from a grocery store that offers Hispanic products.

10. **¡Inténtelo!** = Try it: Try out your new skills and continue to communicate in Spanish. Finally, remember "Donde existe voluntad, hay un camino. = Where there is a will, there is a way."

ELEMENTARY SPANISH CHATBOOK ©SPANISH CHAT COMPANY

LECCIÓN 10

110 CIENTO DIEZ

DIEZ IDEAS PARA PROYECTOS = TEN IDEAS FOR PROJECTS

Here are ten project ideas that will help you keep practicing Spanish:

1. **Juego** = Game: Invent your own board game that practices Spanish vocabulary and phrases. You could also make a matching game or any of the other games from the 10 lessons. Create a crossword puzzle or word search and give it to your friends to practice.

2. **Tarjetas** = Flashcards: Make new flashcards with other vocabulary words such as animals, body parts or more food words. Learn a new phrase each and every day. Play some of the games from the *Elementary Spanish Chatbook* using your new flashcards.

3. **Mantel Individual** = Placemat: Make a placemat decorated with lots of Spanish vocabulary and phrases. Laminate it with clear contact paper to make it more durable. You could also design your own stamp or your very own personal flag.

4. **Cartel** = Poster: Design a poster to practice some of the Spanish words and phrases. Decorate it with lots of bright colors and images. You could also make a bookmark or cut apart your poster to make your own puzzle.

5. **Vídeo Casero** = Home video: Practice a skit in Spanish and then record a movie. Make puppets or recruit friends and family to be a part of your video. You could act out the story of the Three Bears or any other fairy tale. Look at Hispanic Leyendas = Folktales for other ideas. A cooking show would also be fun to record. Tell about the ingredients and give directions in Spanish. Take the viewer on a tour of your home or school in Spanish. Try to sell a product with a Spanish infomercial. There are many possibilities so invent your own idea for a movie in Spanish.

6. **Folleto** = Brochure: You are a travel agent advertising your Spanish-speaking country. Make a brochure, poster or computer presentation trying to convince everyone to come visit. Include the flag, the capital city and some interesting things to do along with some facts about your country

7. **Menú** = Menu: Design your own Spanish menu and describe each item that you are serving. Research menus for ideas.

8. **Días Festivos** = Holidays: Use the holiday guide from pp. 114-116 = ciento catorce hasta ciento dieciséis and celebrate one of the Spanish-speaking holidays.

9. **Libro** = Book: Make your own book in Spanish to practice with the phrases and vocabulary. You could write a story about a Hispanic holiday, a trip or even a book about your typical day. Translating a children's book into Spanish is another idea. Share your story with your family and friends.

10. **Alguna Otra Idea** = Any other idea: Create any other meaningful project that will help you most in your life.

Recorta = Cut out along the dashed lines

ELEMENTARY SPANISH CHATBOOK

CERTIFICADO DE RECONOCIMIENTO

Me llamo: _____

_____ de la maestra o el maestro

La fecha es el _____

LEARN SPANISH TODAY FOR WORK & PLAY

©SPANISH CHAT COMPANY

APENDICE = APPENDIX

RESPUESTAS Y GLOSARIO = ANSWERS AND GLOSSARY

- 🌎 Gracias
- 🌎 Supermercado = Grocery Store Scavenger Hunt
- 🌎 Holidays = Fiestas
- 🌎 Examen: Preguntas y Respuestas = Exam: Questions & Answers
- 🌎 Respuestas = Answers
- 🌎 Frases positivas y Mandatos = Positive Phrases & Commands
- 🌎 Glosario = Glossary Of Words & Phrases From This Book:
    English = Spanish & then Spanish = English
- 🌎 ¿Quieres más? = Want more? Order Form for *Spanish Chatbooks*

GRACIAS = THANK YOU

FROM THE AUTHOR

My *Elementary Spanish Chatbook* is dedicated to the many people around the world that are working very hard to support their families and learn another language. I hope to build bridges of communication and connections in our global society. Now you will be able to speak another language and get to know a new "amigo" or "amiga."

Gracias y saludos to my family and friends, husband, Brad, son Jaden, daughter Elena, my students and future travelers everywhere. Thanks to Indira Engel, Vieva McClure, Gonzalo Baron, Alejandra Rebolledo, Dana Campbell, Curtis Grubb and Wendy Biernbaum for her amazing designs. A big Gracias to Sonia Carbonell for her cartoons. An extra thanks to my parents and grandparents who have been amazing role models for me and take care of my children so I can go on aventuras in Latin America. Thank you for helping me make my dreams become a reality.

To my readers and Spanish students, thank you for taking your time and putting in the effort to learn Spanish. Feel free to visit our Web site www.SpanishChatCompany.com to give us feedback or ask questions. You will love the Spanish Chatshow videos that enhance each lesson. If you have any suggestions or changes for a future edition, just let us know.

I would love to hear testimonials of how this *Elementary Spanish Chatbook* has helped you. Keep practicing and keep smiling.

Aprovecha cada momento. = Take advantage of each moment.
Vale la pena. = It is worth it.
¡Disfruta la aventura! = Enjoy the adventure!
¡Buen Viaje! = Have a nice trip!

Con cariño y sonrisas = with love and smiles,
Tu Maestra Julia = Your teacher Julie

SUPERMERCADO = GROCERY STORE

Go to a Grocery store and try to find the answers to these questions.
Find a store that carries Hispanic items if possible.

¿De qué color son las frutas y las verduras? =

What color are the fruits and vegetables? Try to find these fruits/vegetables and write the color on the line.

1. Nopales _____

2. Dos tipos de Chiles_____ y _____

3. Yuca _____

4. Plátanos _____ (Hint: These are bigger than bananas)

5. Guava o Guayaba _____

6. Alguna otra fruta o verdura de América Latina _____
Some other fruit or vegetable from Latin America (Write the color and name of the fruit)

¿Cuál es el nombre de un dulce? =

What is the name of a sweet? Find the name of these sweet items

7. Chocolate caliente _____ =
Hint: It is either Abuelita o Mamá hot chocolate mix

8. Dos refrescos, gaseosas _____ y _____ =
two refreshments or carbonated drinks

9. Dos jugos _____ y _____ =
two juices

10. Dos Galletas _____ y _____ =
two cookies

11. Dos marcas de papas _____ y _____ =
two brands of chips

12. Algún otro dulce de América Latina _____ =
Some other sweet or candy from Latin America (Write the name of the candy or sweet)

SUPERMERCADO = GROCERY STORE

¿Cuáles son los ingredientes de la comida típica? =
What are the ingredients in typical food? Find these items and list two of the ingredients.

13. Mole: Los ingredientes son _____ y _____ =
stew/sauce

14. 14. Pan Bimbo: Los ingredientes son _____ y
_____ = Bimbo brand bread

15. 15. Tortillas o tostadas: Los ingredientes son _____ y
_____ = tortillas or fried/toasted tortillas

16. 16. Frijoles: Los ingredientes son _____ y
_____ = beans

¿Cuáles son las marcas de otras cosas? =
What are the brand names for other items in the store.

17. La música Mexicana se llama _____ =
Mexican music

18. Una revista o un periódico se llama _____ =
Magazine or newspaper

19. Para lavar ropa se usa _____ =
to wash clothes they use

La panadería =
The bakery. Look for a bakery section or a nearby bakery. Ask these questions directly to an employee if the items are not labeled.

20. ¿Qué tipo de empanadas tiene hoy?_____ =
What type of empanada pasteries do you have today?

21. ¿Cuánto cuesta el pan pequeño? Cuesta $_____. =
How much does a small bread cost?

22. ¿De qué colores son los panes dulces llamados conchas? Las conchas son
_____ y _____. =
What colors are sweet breads that are called seashells?

El restaurante = the restuarant.

23. Vayan a un restaurante Latino y pidan tu comida y bebida en español. = Go to a Latino Restaurant and ask for your food and drink in Spanish.

ELEMENTARY SPANISH CHATBOOK ©SPANISH CHAT COMPANY

DÍAS FESTIVOS = HOLIDAYS

- **Año Nuevo y Nochevieja** = New Year and New Year's Eve is on January 1 and December 31. Many people eat 12 grapes as the clock strikes midnight. Wearing yellow underwear in Peru is a symbol of good luck, while wearing black can mean bad luck. Sweeping out the house symbolizes sweeping out the old; in Cuba, they also throw a bucket of water out the window. In South America, walking around the house or block with suitcases is supposed to help bring travel opportunities, while in Ecuador they hide money around the house. In Chile, they wait for the new year in a graveyard and eat lentils for good luck. In Panamá, Ecuador, Paraguay and Colombia, they make a scarecrow "muñeco" and burn it in a bonfire to symbolize getting rid of the past. Fireworks are common throughout Latin America.
IDEA: Make a poster or act out a play with these traditions.

- **El Día de los Reyes Magos** = The Day of the Three Magi Kings is on January 6. Latino children place their shoes by the door before going to bed. While they sleep the Three Kings, "Melchor, Gaspar y Baltazar" come and leave a gift. Traditionally, children would only get gifts from the Kings and not for Christmas, but now they may get gifts for both holidays. The Rosca/Roscón de Reyes = Cake of the Kings / Panettone is a fruitcake eaten on this holiday. A coin or small plastic baby "Jesus" is often hidden inside the cake. The person that finds the baby has to host the next party. IDEA: Make a King's cake and give a crown to the student that finds the baby. Have students each put one shoe in the hallway and go back to the classroom. Recruit another teacher to put a piece of candy, a sticker, or a small gift inside each shoe.

- **Día de los Enamorados / Día de San Valentín** = Valentine's Day is usually celebrated on February 14. Although, in Colombia, it is in September and Día de Amor y la Amistad = Day of Love and Friendship can also be celebrated in July. It is a day to honor loved ones with flowers, candies and cards. It is also popular to draw names for an "amigo secreto" = secret friend and anonymously give that person notes and gifts for a week IDEA: Draw names for an "amigo secreto" and make cards and notes in Spanish. Use some of the positive phrases from p. 120 = ciento veinte.

- **Carnaval** = Carnival is a Mardi Gras around Ash Wednesday which is usually in February or early March. In Puerto Rico, Cuba and the Dominican Republic, they make elaborate masks and parade to Conga and other Latin music. In Puerto Rico, folks dress as a "Vejigante" with brightly colored spotted outfits and masks with five or more horns. They carry a "veija" = dried, painted cow bladder filled with air like a balloon. IDEA: Make the masks from p. 97 = noventa y siete and have a parade with Conga music. Have students tie a balloon onto a stick or make a maraca from p. 107 = ciento siete.

- **Semana Santa and Pascua** = Holy week and Easter is sometime in March or April. Some Latin Americans go to church every day for this week. Church bells are silenced on Good Friday. During processions in Sevilla, Spain, as many as 50 people carry "pasos" = wooden religious sculptures and others dress in robes of various colors with matching pointed hoods. Parades and parties often are held on Fat Tuesday. In Spain, groups of friends coordinate costumes and dress up in themes. For example, they might all be witches, babies or soccer players. In Copán, Honduras, they use sawdust and flowers to make colorful designs on the streets before the Good Friday parade. Typical foods are: Rosca de Pascua = Easter cake ring, Potaje de la Vigilia = Vigil fasting soup, Ceviche = raw lemon soaked fish, Tortas de Pescado = fish cakes. IDEA: Make Cascarones from p. 37 = treinta y siete and try some Latin American fish recipes.

DÍAS FESTIVOS = HOLIDAYS

- **Día de la Madre** = Mother's Day is celebrated the second Sunday in May in many countries. Although in Spain it is the first Sunday in May and in Paraguay it is always May 15, "Madre Patria" = Mother Nation. May 10 is always Mother's Day in Mexico and El Salvador. Costa Rica honors mothers on August 15 = Assumption of Mary. Panama celebrates on December 8 and Argentina has their Mother's Day in October. IDEA: Make a card in Spanish for your mom, aunt or grandma.

- **Día del Padre** = Father's Day is celebrated in many countries on the 3rd Sunday in June. In Bolivia, Honduras, Uruguay and Spain, it is combined with the Día de San José = Day of St. Joseph. In Argentina, it is August 24 and in Uruguay it is in July. IDEA: Make a card in Spanish for your dad, uncle or grandpa.

- **Día del Niño** = Children's Day is officially November 20 according to the United Nations and is celebrated in Spain on that day but other countries honor a different day. Children throughout Latin America receive a present for this special day and have special activities or even a day off school. In Mexico it is April 30; Bolivia is on April 12 while Colombia and Peru also celebrate in April. June 1 is Nicaragua and Ecuador although Venezuela, Cuba and Panama all honor their children with a special day sometime in July. Uruguay, Chile, Peru, Paraguay, Puerto Rico and Argentina all celebrate in August. September 9 is Children's Day in Costa Rica; September 10 is Honduras while October 1 is El Salvador and Guatemala. Finally, the Dominican Republic have their day for children in December. IDEA: Draw the flag of each country on the calendar and send positive thoughts to the children of that country on that day or do a service learning project to help a child on each Children's Day.

- **Día del Maestro** = Teacher's Day is celebrated on many different days. In Mexico, it is on May 15 although the dates vary throughout Latin America. IDEA: Make a Spanish card or bring flowers to your favorite teacher.

- **Cinco de Mayo** = May 5 is a celebration of the victory of one Mexican battle against the French in 1862. Cinco de Mayo is actually a bigger celebration in the United States, demonstrating Mexican-American pride. IDEA: Have a parade for Cinco de Mayo and ask everyone to wear red, white and green. Make serapes = scarves out of grocery sacks, make maracas from p. 107 = ciento siete and dance to the song on p. 11 = once "El Alfabeto."

- **Día de Independencia** = Independence Day is one of the biggest celebrations in each country, with parades and festivals in the town square. For example, Independence Day in México is September 16. (Many people confuse this with Cinco de Mayo.) Independence Day in Guatemala, El Salvador, Honduras, Nicaragua and Costa Rica is September 15. Find the exact dates listed on your mini calendar from p. 69 = sesenta y nueve. IDEA: Have a parade for Independence Day for a Spanish-speaking country and make flags and banners to represent the country that you have chosen.

DÍAS FESTIVOS = HOLIDAYS

- **Día de la Hispanidad** = Day of the Hispanic world honors the discovery of the Américas on October 12, 1492, by explorers such as Cristóbal Colón = Christopher Columbus. The day is also called "Día de la Raza" = "Day of the Race." In Argentina they call it "Día del Respeto a la Diversidad Cultural" = "Day of Respect of Cultural Diversity." In Chile they call it "Día del Encuentro de Dos Mundos" = "Day of Encounter (Discovery) of 2 Worlds." In Uruguay, they celebrate "Día de las Américas" = "Day of the Americas" on April 12. IDEA: Have a potluck during Hispanic Heritage month and invite and interview Latinos in your community.

- **Día de Brujas** = Halloween on October 31 is not a traditional Latin American holiday. However, in some places such as Chile, Colombia and Mexico, children have been influenced by Hollywood and are starting to ask neighbors for candies by saying "Dulce o Truco" = "Sweet or Trick." In Costa Rica, some people now go to costume parties at the discos. It is also known as "Víspera del Día de Todos los Santos = Eve of All Saints' Day." IDEA: Make a skeleton by gluing pasta on black paper and label the body parts with a white crayon. Draw a haunted house and label the furniture and Halloween icons in Spanish. Did you know that Murciélago = bat is one of the only Spanish words that includes all of the vowels?

- **Día de los Muertos** = Day of the Dead is celebrated November 1–2 primarily in Mexico, but some other places in Latin America also honor their loved ones. This is essentially like Memorial Day. Families leave a trail of marigold flowers from their house to the cemetary in the hopes that the souls are able to find their way back home for one day. They build ofrendas = altars with sugar skulls to honor the deceased. IDEA: Try making your own ofrenda.

- **Día de Acción de Gracias** = Thanksgiving is celebrated in the United States of America and Canada on the fourth Thursday in November. This is not a Latin American holiday. IDEA: Translate a menu of your typical holiday dinner into Spanish. IDEA: Make a place mat with Spanish words & phrases.

- **Las Posadas** = The Inns is celebrated in Mexico, Guatemala and Colombia from December 16-24. The nine days before Christmas symbolize the nine months before Jesus' birth. Each family commemorates the occasiona differently, but many times they will sing villancicos = traditional holiday songs and gather together for meals with friends and relatives. Some groups of neighbors knock on door after door and are turned away by each "innkeeper." At the final house, they are let in for the fiesta = party usually with a star piñata The process is repeated for nine nights in a row with a different family hosting each evening. IDEA: Make a piñata using a balloon. Papier-mâché it by dipping newspapers into a mixture of glue and water. Let it dry and paint it. Fill it with candy and hang it from a tree. Hit it with a stick to break it open saying, "dale, dale, dale." = "give it, give it, give it."

- **Nochebuena and Navidad** = Christmas Eve and Christmas Day is celebrated on December 24-25 throughout Latin America and Spain. Poinsettias are used as decorations. This is an important Christian holiday with celebrations at churches and family dinners. Usually the figure of the baby Jesus is not placed into the manger until Christmas Day. Papá Noel = Santa Claus brings gifts and you will see many lights and decorations. Puerto Rico celebrates from November until February. IDEA: Research the stories and legends of the Poinsettia flower. Make poinsettias out of construction paper and act out the story. Make a holiday card or gift for someone special.

EXAMEN FOR THE ELEMENTARY SPANISH CHATBOOK

Try taking this examen = exam either orally or written. Practice asking and answering these question with native Spanish speakers and other students from your class.

LECCIÓN = LESSON	PREGUNTA = QUESTION	RESPUESTA = ANSWER
1	¿Cómo te llamas?	Me llamo...
2	¿Cómo estás?	Estoy...
3	¿A tí te gusta un deporte?	A mí me gusta...
4	¿Cuántos años tienes?	Tengo...años.
5	¿Cómo dices los miembros de tu familia en español?	Digo...
6	¿Cuándo es tu cumpleaños?	Mi cumpleaños es el...de...
7	¿Qué clima hace hoy?	Hace...
8	¿Quieres algo para la escuela?	Sí quiero...
9	¿Cuáles colores ves aquí?	Veo...
10	¿Qué vas a comer?	Voy a comer...

RESPUESTAS = ANSWERS

ANSWERS FOR LESSON 2 CULTURA #26

#3 is false "If you order a "Tortilla con Queso" in Spain, you would get something like a quesadilla with a soft flour taco shell" is false because a Tortilla con Queso in Spain is also called a Tortilla Patata con Queso = A potato omelet with cheese. It is more like a fritatta or an egg omelette made out of two onions, four potatoes and six eggs. Queso = cheese, Jamón = Ham, Chorizo = sausage. Other ingredients are sometimes added.

ANSWERS FOR LESSON 3 CULTURA #36

#2 is false "The Aztecs had a dream that they should build Mexico City where they found an eagle holding a cactus in its mouth" is false because the Aztecs dream said Mexico City should be built on the spot where an eagle is STANDING on a cactus holding a SNAKE in its mouth. This is the symbol in the center of the Mexican flag.

ANSWERS FOR LESSON 4 CULTURA #46

#1 is false "The five stars on the flag of Honduras represent the five official holidays celebrated in Honduras, one of which is Children's Day, September 10" is false because the five stars represent the five original Central American countries of Guatemala, El Salvador, Honduras, Nicaragua and Costa Rica. The blue stripes represent the Pacific ocean and the Caribbean sea. Children's day on September 10 is a national holiday with presents for the kids and celebrations at school instead of classes.

ANSWERS FOR LESSON 5 CULTURA #56

#3 is false "It takes large ships about two hours to cross the Panama canal" is false because it takes about 8-10 hours to pass through all 12 locks. Each lock adjusts the water level to allow the ship to continue passage. The average cost for a commercial vessel is about $120,000. The Panama canal saves time and money for the 15,000 ships a year that would otherwise have to go into the icy waters for a three week journey around South America.

ANSWERS FOR LESSON 6 CULTURA #66

#2 is false 'In Venezuela, the world's highest waterfall is named Angel Falls because at 3,212 feet it is near the Angels" is false because it is named after Jimmie Angel, the first pilot to fly over it. The indigenous name is Kerepakupai Vená meaning, "waterfall of the deepest place."

RESPUESTAS = ANSWERS

ANSWERS FOR LESSON 7 TODOS #72

1. F 2. D 3. H 4. G
5. B 6. A 7. C 8. E

ANSWERS FOR LESSON 7 CULTURA #76

#3 is false "Machu Picchu, Peru, is a city shaped like a jaguar built on top of a mountain. Try a bite of cuy = roasted guinea pig at the restaurant." is false because the city is shaped like a condor bird not a jaguar. Some tourists are able to climb to the top of the nearby mountain and overlook the city to see how they Incans built Machu Picchu around the year 1450. It was incredibly built on top of the mountain in the shape of the condor. The stones fit together so perfectly that they did not need to put mortar in between them. Cuy which is fried or roasted guinea pig is served at many restaurants throughout Peru.

ANSWERS FOR LESSON 8 CULTURA #86

#1 is false "Uruguay has never won the Copa Mundial en fútbol = World Cup in soccer." is false because Uruguay won the soccer World Cup in 1930 and also in 1950.

ANSWERS FOR LESSON 9 CULTURA #96

#2 is false "The coquí frog in Puerto Rico sings/croaks all day long and is quiet all night." is false because the coquí frog actually sings from dusk to dawn which is all night long. Tourists that are not used to the sound sometimes complain but the frog is a mascot for the islanders.

ANSWERS FOR LESSON 10 CULTURA #106

#1 is false "Equatorial Guinea is in one of the smallest countries in Africa located just across the ocean from Spain." is false because it is one of the smallest countries and the only Spanish-speaking country in Africa, but it is not across the ocean from Spain. (Morocco, Africa, is across the Strait of Gibraltar from Spain.) Equatorial Guinea is located on the Atlantic Ocean in West Central Africa-, south of Cameroon and North of Gabon.

POSITIVE AFFIRMATIONS

PICK 3 OF THESE THAT DESCRIBE YOU. USE A NEW PHRASE EACH DAY! FIND THE ENGLISH TRANSLATIONS BEFORE THE TABLE OF CONTENTS.

SEA AMABLE. = BE KIND.	YO SOY...TU ERES...ELLA ES...ÉL ES...
¡Bien hecho!	admirable
¡Brilliante!	amable
¡Buen trabajo!	asombroso / asombrosa
¡Espectacular!	bonito / bonita
¡Estupendo! / ¡Estupenda!	bueno / buena
¡Excelente!	cortés
Excepcional!	especial
¡Extraordinario! / ¡Extraordinaria!	éxitoso / éxitosa
¡Fabuloso! / ¡Fabulosa!	fascinante
¡Fantástico! / ¡Fantástica!	inteligente
¡Fenomenal!	listo / lista
¡Genial!	organizado / organizada
¡Impresionante!	orgulloso / orgullosa
¡Increíble!	paciente
¡Magnífico! / ¡Magnífica!	precioso /preciosa
¡Marvilloso! / ¡Maravillosa!	puntual
¡Muy bien!	respetuoso / respetuosa
¡Perfecto! / ¡Perfecta!	responsable
¡Qué bien!	simpático
¡Qué chévere!	un buen amigo / una buena amiga
¡Ideal!	un buen estudiante / una buena estudiante
¡Sobresaliente!	un campeón / una campeóna
¡Sensacional!	un ganador / una ganadora
¡Super!	único / única
¡Superior!	valiente

ELEMENTARY SPANISH CHATBOOK ©SPANISH CHAT COMPANY

CLASSROOM COMMANDS

to one student / more than one student

Abre / Abren = open	**Levántate / Levántense** = stand up
Anda / Anden = walk	**Mira / Miren** = look
Borra / Borren = erase	**Muestra / Muestren** = show
Salta / Salten = jump	**Párate / Párense** = stop
Busca / Busquen = look for	**Pasa / Pasen** = pass
Canta / Canten = sing	**Pon / Pongan** = put
Cierra / Cierren = close	**Practica / Practiquen** = practice
Cocina / Cocinen = cook	**Pregunta / Pregunten** = ask
Colorea / Coloreen = color	**Quita / Quiten** = take off
Contesta / Contesten = answer	**Recoge / Recojan** = pick up
Corta / Corten = cut	**Recorta / Recorten** = cut out
Cuenta / Cuenten = count	**Repite / Repitan** = repeat
Da / Den = give	**Responde / Respondan** = respond
Da / Den un saltito = hop	**Saca / Saquen** = take out
Date / Dense una vuelta = turn around	**Sal / Salgan** = leave
Di / Digan = say	**Señala / Señalen** = point to
Dibuja / Dibujen = draw	**Siéntate / Siéntense** = sit down
Dobla / Doblen = fold, turn	**Sigue / Sigan** = follow
Entra / Entren = enter	**Suma / Sumen** = add up
Escoge / Escojan = choose	**Termina / Terminen** = finish, end
Escribe / Escriban = write	**Tira / Tiren** = throw
Escucha / Escuchen = listen	**Toca / Toquen** = touch
Habla / Hablen = talk	**Toma / Tomen** = take
Intenta / Intenten = try	**Trae / Traigan** = bring
Juega / Jueguen = play	**Ve / Vayan** = go
Lee / Lean = read	**Ven / Vengan** = come

ELEMENTARY SPANISH CHATBOOK

GLOSARIO: ENGLISH = SPANISH

a = **un(a)** (pp. 30, 70)

actions = **acciones** (p. 82)

address = **dirección** (p. 139)

afternoon(s) = **tarde(s)** (p. 10)

a lot = **mucha/o(s)** (pp. 10, 40, 50)

alphabet = **alfabeto** (p. 11)

already = **ya** (p. 30)

am (changing) = **estoy** (pp. 20, 138)

am (permanent) = **soy** (pp. 16, 138-139)

and = **y** (p. 20)

animal(s) (p. 40) = **animal(es)**

answer(s) = **respuesta(s)** (pp. 118-119)

are (more than 1 subject—changing) = **están** (p. 138)

are (more than 1 subject—permanent) = **son** (pp. 112-113,, 138)

are (one subject—changing) = **estás** (pp. 20, 138)

are (one subject—permanent) = **eres** (pp. 60, 138)

around = **alrededor** (p. 72)

ask for = **pedir** (p. 80)

April = **abril** (p. 60)

art = **arte** (pp. 17, 27, 37, 47, 57, 67, 77, 87, 97, 107)

August = **agosto** (p. 60)

Aztec = **Azteca** (pp. 36, 39, 67)

bad = **mal** (pp. 20, 70)

backpack = **mochila** (p. 85)

baseball = **béisbol** (p. 30)

basketball = **baloncesto** (p. 30)

bathroom = **baño** (p. 80)

beans = **frijoles** (p. 45)

because = **por, porque** (p. 50, 139)

black = **negra/o(s)** (p. 90)

blue = **azul(es)** (p. 90)

book(s) = **libro(s)** (pp. 34, 64, 80, 94)

bow-wow = **guau, guau** (p. 50)

Bingo = **lotería** (p. 45)

birthday = **cumpleaños** (p. 60)

breakfast = **desayuno** (p. 100)

brother = **hermano** (p. 50)

brown = **café(s)** (p. 90)

by = **por, de** (p. 50, 60, 100)

calendar = **calendario** (pp. 39, 60, 61, 69)

cap = **gorra** (p. 90)

careful = **cuidado** (p. 70)

cat (female) = **gata/o(s)** (p. 50)

Central America = **América Central** (pp. 46, 56)

cereal = **cereal** (p. 100)

chair = **silla** (p. 80)

change = **cambien** (p. 32)

chicken = **pollo** (p. 100)

children = **niña/o(s)** (pp. 8, 28, 32, 69, 115)

clothing = **ropa** (pp. 90, 95)

code = **código** (p. 49)

GLOSARIO: ENGLISH = SPANISH

cold = **frío** (p. 70)

color (the action) = **colorea** (p. 80)

colors = **colores** (p. 90)

commands = **mandatos** (p. 5, 121)

Cook it! = **¡Cocínalo!** (pp. 18, 28, 38, 48, 58, 68, 78, 88, 98, 108)

crayons = **crayones** (p. 80)

cut / cut out = **corta / recorta** (pp. 80)

dad = **papá** (pp. 12, 50)

dance = **bailar** (p. 30)

day(s) = **día(s)** (p. 10, 60, 80)

December = **diciembre** (p. 60)

dessert = **postre** (p. 100)

dice = **dados** (p. 62)

dinner = **cena** (p. 100)

dog = **perro** (p. 50)

do (I) = **hago** (pp. 70, 138)

do (more than one subject) = **hacen** (p. 138)

Do it! = **¡Hazlo!** (pp. 17, 27, 37, 47, 57, 67, 77, 87, 97, 107)

Do you like...? = **¿A tí te gusta...?** (pp. 30, 138)

Do you have...? = **¿Tienes...?** (p. 40)

does (informal you) = **haces** (p. 138)

does (one subject) = **hace** (pp. 70, 138)

drawings = **dibujos** (p. 65)

duck = **pato** (p. 22)

eight = **8 ocho** (p. 40)

eighteen = **18 dieciocho** (p. 40)

eighty = **80 ochenta** (p. 40)

elementary = **primaría** (p. 139)

eleven = **once** (p. 40)

English = **inglés** (pp. 14, 24, 44, 54, 74, 84, 104)

equal = **igual** (p. 72)

erase = **borra** (p. 80)

evening(s) = **tarde(s)** (p. 10)

everyone = **todos** (p. 55)

everything = **todo** (p. 55)

exam = **examen** (p. 117)

example(s) = **ejemplo(s)** (p. 59)

face(s) = **cara(s)** (p. 29)

false = **falso** (p. 105)

family = **familia** (pp. 50-51)

farmer = **granjera/o** (p. 22)

fashion = **moda** (p. 92)

favorite = **favorita/o** (pp. 33, 61)

February = **febrero** (p. 60)

few = **poca/o(s)** (pp. 40, 70)

fifteen = **15 quince** (p. 40)

fifty = **50 cincuenta** (p. 40)

fingers = **dedos** (p. 105)

Finish it! = **¡Termínalo!** (pp. 19, 29, 39, 49, 59, 69, 79, 89, 99, 109)

five = **5 cinco** (p. 40)

GLOSARIO: ENGLISH = SPANISH

four = **4 cuatro** (p. 40)

fourteen = **14 catorce** (p. 40)

forty = **40 cuarenta** (p. 40)

flag(s) = **bandera(s)** (pp. 26, 36, 46, 56, 66, 76, 86, 96, 106)

food = **comida** (pp. 18, 28, 38, 48, 58, 68 78, 88, 92, 98, 108)

football = **fútbol americano** (p. 30)

for = **por/para** (pp. 50/80)

friend(s) = **amiga/o(s)** (p. 10)

Friday = **viernes** (p. 60)

from = **de** (pp. 60, 100)

fruits = **frutas** (p. 100)

Play it! = **¡Juégalo!** (p. 15, 25, 35, 45, 55, 65, 75, 85, 95, 105)

glossary = **glosario** (pp. 122-137)

glue = **pegamento** (p. 80)

go (I) = **voy** (pp. 100, 138)

go (informal you) = **vas** (pp. 100, 138)

go (more than one subject) = **van** (p. 138)

goes (one subject) = **va** (p. 138)

good = **buena/o(s)** (pp. 10, 50, 90, 100)

goodbye = **adiós** (p. 10)

goose = **ganzo** (p. 22)

grandparents = **abuelos** (p. 50)

gray = **gris(es)** (p. 90)

great = **buena/o(s)** (pp. 10, 50, 90, 100)

green = **verde(s)** (p. 90)

greetings = **saludos** (p. 20)

Guess it! = **¡Adivínalo!** (p. 79)

hamburger = **hamburguesa** (p. 100)

hand = **mano** (p. 80)

happy = **feliz** (p. 20)

has (one subject) = **tiene** (pp. 59, 113, 138)

have (I) = **tengo** (pp. 40, 138)

have (more than one subject) = **tienen** (p. 138)

have (informal you) = **tienes** (pp. 40, 138)

he = **él** (p. 59)

head = **cabeza** (p. 22)

heat = **calor** (p. 70)

hello = **hola** (p. 10)

help = **ayuda** (p. 80)

here = **aquí** (pp. 42, 90)

high school = **secundaría** (p. 139)

holidays = **días festivos** (pp. 37, 69, 114-116)

homework = **tarea** (pp. 19, 29, 39, 49, 59, 69, 79, 89, 99, 109)

hour = **hora** (p. 139)

house = **casa** (p. 50)

how/what = **cómo** (pp. 10, 12, 20, 139)

how many = **cuánta/o(s)** (pp. 40, 139)

how much = **cuánta/o(s)** (pp. 40. 139)

I = **yo** (pp. 41, 50, 80, 90, 100)

I am...(changing) = **estoy** (p. 20)

GLOSARIO: ENGLISH = SPANISH

I am...(permanent) = **soy** (pp. 16, 138-139)

I am called... = **Me llamo...** (pp. 10, 21, 128)

I like... = **A mí me gusta...** (pp. 30, 138)

I love you. = **Te quiero.** (p. 50)

I say... = **Yo digo...** (p. 50)

ice cream = **helado** (p. 100)

if = **si** (p. 82)

in = **en** (p. 50)

in order to = **para** (p. 80)

is (one subject—changing) = **está** (pp. 59, 138)

is (one subject—permanent) = **es** (pp. 60, 80, 138-9)

it = **lo** (p. 80)

It's your turn. = **Te toca a ti.** (p. 75)

jacket = **chaqueta** (p. 90)

January = **enero** (p. 60)

judge = **juez** (p. 102)

June = **junio** (p. 60)

July = **julio** (p. 60)

kid(s) = **niña/o(s)** (pp. 8, 28, 32, 69, 115)

later = **luego** (p. 10)

leader = **líder** (p. 32)

less = **menos** (pp. 40, 42)

Let's go! = **¡Vámonos!** (p. 50)

lie (not true) = **mentira** (p. 105)

little (amount) = **poca/o(s)** (pp. 40, 70)

little (size) = **pequeña/o(s)** (p. 69)

Look at it! = **¡Míralo** (p. 16, 26, 36, 46, 56, 66, 76, 86, 96, 106)

lottery = **lotería** (p. 45)

luck = **suerte** (p. 62)

lunch = **almuerzo** (p. 100)

make (I) = **hago** (pp. 70, 138)

makes (informal you) = **haces** (p. 138)

make (more than one subject) = **hacen** (p. 138)

makes (one subject) = **hace** (pp. 70, 138)

many = **mucha/o(s)** (pp. 10, 40, 50)

map = **mapa** (pp. 35, 80)

March = **marzo** (p. 60)

math = **matemáticas** (p. 52)

May = **mayo** (p. 60)

meat = **carne** (p. 100)

meow = **miau** (p. 50)

microphone = **micrófono** (p. 92)

milk = **leche** (p. 100)

mistakes = **faltas** (p. 80)

model = **modelo** (p. 92)

mom = **mamá** (pp. 12, 50)

Monday = **lunes** (p. 60)

more = **más** (pp. 40, 42)

morning = **mañana** (p. 79)

much = **mucha/o(s)** (pp. 10, 40, 50)

ELEMENTARY SPANISH CHATBOOK ©SPANISH CHAT COMPANY

GLOSARIO: ENGLISH = SPANISH

my = **mi** (pp. 50, 59)

My name is... = **Me llamo...** (pp. 10, 21, 138)

nap = **siesta** (p. 100)

Nice to meet you. = **Mucho gusto.** (p. 10)

night(s) = **noche(s)** (pp. 10, 100)

nine = **9 nueve** (p. 40)

nineteen = **19 diecinueve** (p. 40)

ninety = **90 noventa** (p. 40)

November = **noviembre** (p. 60)

no = **no** (pp. 12, 80, 100)

nothing = **nada** (p. 50)

now = **ahora, ya** (p. 30)

number(s) = **número(s)** (pp. 40, 41, 52)

October = **octubre** (p. 60)

one = **1 uno** (p. 40)

one hundred = **100 cien** (p. 40)

only = **sólo** (p. 70)

of = **de** (pp. 60, 100)

or = **o** (pp. 29, 40, 42, 61, 82, 105)

orange = **anaranjada/o(s)** (p. 90)

order (action) = **pedir** (p. 80)

other(s) = **otra/o(s)** (p. 93)

pairs = **pares** (p. 75)

pants = **pantalones** (p. 90)

paper = **papel** (p. 80)

pardon = **perdón** (p. 15)

party = **fiesta** (p. 100)

Pass it on. = **Pásalo.** (p. 92)

pencil = **lápiz** (p. 80)

pink = **rosa(s)** (p. 90)

please = **por favor** (p. 50)

pleasure = **gusto** (p. 10)

poor little girl/boy = **pobrecita/o** (p. 20)

potatoes = **papas** (p. 100)

Practice it! = **¡Practícalo!** (p. 14, 24, 34, 44, 54, 64, 74, 84, 94, 104)

prepared = **preparados** (p. 30)

primary = **primaría** (p. 139)

purple = **morada/o(s)** (p. 90)

put = **pon**(one subject)/**ponen** (two or more) (p. 55)

questions = **preguntas** (p. 139)

rain / it rains = **lluvia / llueve** (pp. 67, 70)

raise up = **levanta** (p. 80)

Read it! = **¡Léelo!** (p. 13, 23, 33, 43, 53, 63, 73, 80, 83, 93, 103)

ready = **listos** (p. 30)

red = **roja/o(s)** (p. 90)

Repeat it! = **¡Repítelo!** (pp. 10, 20, 30, 40, 50, 60, 70, 80, 90, 100)

rice = **arroz** (p. 100)

roll (the dice) = **tiras los dados** (p. 62)

room = **cuarto** (p. 99)

row = **raya** (p. 25)

GLOSARIO: ENGLISH = SPANISH

run = **correr** (p. 30)

sad = **triste** (p. 20)

salad = **ensalada** (p. 100)

same = **igual** (p. 72)

Saturday = **sábado** (p. 60)

say (I) = **digo** (pp. 50, 138)

say (informal you) = **dices** (pp. 50, 138)

say (more than one subject) = **dicen** (pp. 50, 138)

says (one subject) = **dice** (pp. 50, 138)

school = **escuela** (pp. 80-81)

scissors = **tijeras** (p. 80)

secondary = **secundaría** (p. 139)

secret = **secreto** (p. 42)

see (I) = **veo** (p. 90)

see (more than one subject) = **ven** (p. 138)

see (you—informal) = **ves** (p. 90)

see you (until) = **hasta** (p. 10)

sees (one subject) = **ve** (p. 138)

September = **septiembre** (p. 60)

seven = **7 siete** (p. 40)

seventeen = **17 diecisiete** (p. 40)

seventy = **70 setenta** (p. 40)

she = **ella** (p. 59)

shirt = **camisa** (p. 90)

shoes = **zapatos** (p. 90)

shorts = **pantalones cortos** (p. 90)

show = **desfile** (p. 92)

ski = **esquiar** (p. 59)

sick girl/boy = **enferma/o** (p. 20)

signs, sign language = **señas** (p. 82)

Sing it! = **¡Cántalo!** (pp. 11, 21, 31, 41, 51, 61, 71, 81, 91, 101)

sister = **hermana** (p. 50)

sit down = **siéntate** (p. 80)

six = **6 seis** (p. 40)

sixteen = **16 diciséis** (p. 40)

sixty = **60 sesenta** (p. 40)

skirt = **falda** (p. 90)

small (size) = **pequeña/o(s)** (p. 69)

small (amount) = **poca/o(s)** (pp. 40, 70)

smart = **listos** (p. 30)

snow / it snows = **nieve / nieva** (p. 70)

snowballs = **bolas de nieve** (p. 70)

soccer = **fútbol** (p. 30)

socks = **calcetines** (p. 90)

some = **unos(as)** (p. 70)

something = **algo** (p. 80)

sorry = **perdón** (p. 15)

South America = **América del Sur** (pp. 66, 76, 78-79, 86)

Spain = **España** (p. 26)

Spanish = **español** (pp. 50, 139)

sport(s) = **deporte(s)** (pp. 30-31)

stand up = **levanta** (p. 80)

ELEMENTARY SPANISH CHATBOOK ©SPANISH CHAT COMPANY

GLOSARIO: ENGLISH = SPANISH

steak = **bistec** (p. 100)

store = **tienda** (p. 99)

strawberry = **fresa** (p. 100)

student(s) = **estudiante(s)** (p. 85)

study (I) = **estudio** (p. 139)

study (you) = **estudias** (p. 139)

style = **estilo** (p. 95)

sun = **sol** (p. 70)

Sunday = **domingo** (p. 60)

supermarket = **supermercado** (p. 112)

supper = **cena** (p. 100)

swim = **nadar** (p. 30)

swimsuit = **traje de baño** (p. 90)

table = **mesa** (p. 80)

take = **toma** (p. 55)

take out = **saca** (p. 80)

teacher(s) female/male = **maestra/o(s)** (pp. 12, 21, 82)

team = **equipo** (p. 65)

telephone = **teléfono** (p. 139)

ten = **10 diez** (p. 40)

thank you very much = **muchas gracias** (p. 50, 111)

the = **el/la/las/los** (pp. 30, 50, 60, 80, 90, 100)

they = **ellos** (p. 138)

three = **3 tres** (p. 40)

thirteen = **13 trece** (p. 40)

thirty = **30 treinta** (p. 40)

this = **esto** (p. 139)

throw = **tira** (p. 62)

thousand = **mil** (p. 60)

Thursday = **jueves** (p. 60)

tired girl/boy = **cansada/o** (p. 20)

to = **a/de/para** (pp. 50, 60, 80, 100)

to be (changing) = **estar** (Lesson 2 & p. 138)

to be (permanent) = **ser** (Lesson 6 & p. 138)

to be called/named = **llamar** (Lesson 1 & p. 138)

to do = **hacer** (Lesson 7 & p. 138)

to eat = **comer** (p. 100)

to go = **ir** (Lesson 10 & pp. 80, 138)

to have = **tener** (Lesson 4 & p. 138)

to like = **gustar** (Lesson 3 & p. 138)

to make = **hacer** (Lesson 7 & p. 138)

to say = **decir** (Lesson 5, & p. 138)

to see = **ver** (Lesson 9 & p. 138)

to take = **tomar** (p. 100)

to travel = **viajar** (p. 59)

to want = **querer** (Lesson 8 & p. 138)

today = **hoy** (p. 60, 70)

tomorrow = **mañana** (p. 79)

tourists = **turistas** (p. 35)

there is/are = **hay** (p. 15)

three = **tres** (p. 25, 40)

through = **por** (p. 50)

ELEMENTARY SPANISH CHATBOOK ©SPANISH CHAT COMPANY

GLOSARIO: ENGLISH = SPANISH

thousand = **mil** (p. 60)

Tuesday = **martes** (p. 60)

truth = **verdad** (p. 105)

Try it! = **¡Inténtalo!**
(pp. 12, 22, 32, 42, 52, 62, 72, 82, 92, 102)

twelve = **12 doce** (p. 40)

twenty = **20 veinte** (p. 40)

two = **2 dos** (p. 40)

until = **hasta** (p. 10)

use = **usa** (p. 80)

vacation = **vacaciones** (p. 80)

vegetables = **verduras** (p. 100)

verbos (chart) = **verbos** (p. 138)

very = **muy** (p. 20)

violet = **violeta(s)** (p. 90)

visit = **visitar** (p. 35)

want (I) = **quiero** (pp. 50, 80, 138)

want (more than one subject) = **quieren** (p. 138)

want (you—informal) = **quieres** (pp. 80, 138)

wants (one subject) = **quiere** (p. 138)

wash = **lava** (p. 90)

Wash them! = **¡Lávalos!** (p. 91)

weather = **clima** (p. 70)

Wednesday = **miércoles** (p. 60)

well = **bien** (p. 20)

welcome = **bienvenida/o(s)** (p. 50)

what = **qué/cómo/cuál**
(pp. 10, 12, 20, 60, 70, 90, 100, 129, 139)

What is your name? = **¿Cómo te llamas?** (p. 10)

when = **cuándo** (p. 60)

where = **dónde** (p. 139)

which = **cuál(es)** (pp. 61, 90, 139)

white = **blanca/o(s)** (p. 90)

who = **quién** (p. 139)

why = **por qué** (p. 13)

windy = **viento** (p. 70)

will be = **será** (p. 79)

with = **con** (pp. 80, 100)

world = **mundo** (p. 72)

write = **escribe** (p. 80)

year(s) = **año(s)** (pp. 40, 60)

yellow = **amarilla/o(s)** (p. 90)

yes = **sí** (pp. 12, 71, 80)

yogurt = **yogur** (p. 100)

you (informal) = **tú** (pp. 20, 50)

you (formal) = **usted** (p. 39)

you all (formal) = **ustedes** (p. 139)

you like = **A tí te gusta...** (pp. 30, 138)

you are called = **te llamas** (pp. 10, 138)

You're welcome. = **De nada.** (p. 50)

your (informal) = **tu(s)** (p. 42, 52, 60, 139)

zero = **0 cero** (p. 40)

ELEMENTARY SPANISH CHATBOOK

GLOSARIO: SPANISH = ENGLISH

a = to (p. 50)

a mí me gusta... = I like... (pp. 30, 138)

¿A tí te gusta...? = Do you like...? (pp. 30, 138)

abril = April (p. 60)

abuelos = grandparents (p. 50)

acciones = actions (p. 82)

adiós = goodbye (p. 10)

¡Adivínalo! = Guess it! (p. 79)

agosto = August (p. 60)

ahora = now (p. 90)

alfabeto = alphabet (p. 11)

algo = something (p. 80)

almuerzo = lunch (p. 100)

alrededor = around (p. 72)

amarilla/o(s) = yellow (p. 90)

América del Sur = South America (pp. 66, 76, 78-79, 86)

América Central = Central America (pp. 46, 56)

amiga/o(s) = friend(s) (p. 10)

anaranjada/o(s) = orange (p. 90)

animal(es) = animal(s) (p. 40)

año(s) = year(s) (p. 40, 60)

aquí = here (pp. 42, 90)

arroz = rice (p. 100)

arte = art (pp. 17, 27, 37, 47, 57, 67, 77, 87, 97, 107)

ayuda = help (p. 80)

azul(es) = blue (p. 90)

Azteca = Aztec (p. 36, 39, 67)

bailar = dance (p. 30)

baloncesto = basketball (p. 30)

bandera(s) = flag(s) (pp. 26, 36, 46, 56, 66, 76, 86, 96, 106)

baño = bathroom (p. 80)

béisbol = baseball (p. 30)

bien = well/fine (p. 20)

bienvenida/o(s) = welcome (p. 50)

bistec = steak (p. 100)

blanca/o(s) = white (p. 90)

bolas de nieve = snowballs (p. 70)

borra = erase (p. 80)

buena/o(s) = good/great (pp. 10, 50. 70, 100)

cabeza = head (p. 22)

café(s) = brown (p. 90)

calcetines = socks (p. 90)

calor = heat (p. 70)

calendario = calendar (pp. 39, 60, 61, 69)

cambien = change (p. 32)

camisa = shirt (p. 90)

¡Cántalo! = Sing it! (pp. 11, 21, 31, 41, 51, 61, 71, 81, 91, 101)

cansada/o(s) = tired girl/boy (p. 20)

GLOSARIO: SPANISH = ENGLISH

cara(s) = face(s) (p. 29)

carne = meat (p. 100)

casa = house (p. 50)

catorce = 14 fourteen (p. 40)

cena = dinner/supper (p. 100)

cereal = cereal (p. 100)

cero = 0 zero (p. 40)

chaqueta = jacket (p. 90)

cien = 100 one hundred (p. 40)

cinco = 5 five (p. 40)

cincuenta = 50 fifty (p. 40)

clima = weather (pp. 70-71)

¡Cocínalo! = Cook it! (pp. 18, 28, 38, 48, 58, 68, 78, 88, 98, 108)

código = code (p. 49)

colorea = color (the action) (p. 80)

colores = colors (p. 90)

comer = to eat (p. 100)

comida = food (pp. 18, 28, 38, 48, 58, 68 78, 88, 92, 98, 108)

cómo = how/what (pp. 10, 12, 20, 139)

¿Cómo te llamas? = What is your name? (p. 10)

con = with (pp. 80, 100)

correr = run (p. 30)

corta = cut (p. 80)

crayones = crayons (p. 80)

cuál(es) = which, what (pp. 61, 90, 139)

cuánta/o(s) = how many / how much (pp. 40, 139)

cuándo = when (pp. 60, 139)

cuarenta = 40 forty (p. 40)

cuarto = room, fourth (p. 99)

cuatro = 4 four (p. 40)

cuidado = careful (p. 70)

cumpleaños = birthday (p. 60)

dados = dice (p. 62)

de = from, of, to, by (pp. 60, 100)

de nada = you're welcome (p. 50)

decir = to say (Lesson 5 & p. 138)

dedos = fingers (p. 105)

deporte(s) = sport(s) (pp. 30-31)

desayuno = breakfast (p. 100)

desfile = show, parade (p. 92)

día(s) = day(s) (p. 10, 60, 80)

días festivos = holidays (pp. 37, 69, 114-116)

dibujos = drawings (p. 65)

diciembre = December (p. 60)

dices = say (informal you) (pp. 50, 138)

dicen = say (more than one subject) (pp. 50, 138)

dice = says (one subject) (pp. 50, 138)

ELEMENTARY SPANISH CHATBOOK

GLOSARIO: SPANISH = ENGLISH

diecinueve = 19 nineteen (p. 40)

dieciocho = 18 eighteen (p. 40)

dieciséis = 16 sixteen (p. 40)

diecisiete = 17 seventeen (p. 40)

diez = 10 ten (p. 40)

digo = say (I) (pp. 50, 138)

dirección = address (p. 139)

doce = 12 twelve (p. 40)

domingo = Sunday (p. 60)

dónde = where (p. 139)

dos = 2 two (p. 40)

ejemplo(s) = example(s) (p. 59)

el = the (pp. 30, 50, 60, 80, 90, 100)

él = he (p. 59)

ella = she (p. 59)

ellos = they (p. 138)

en = in (p. 50)

enero = January (p. 60)

enferma/o(s) = sick girl/boy (p. 20)

ensalada = salad (p. 100)

equipo = team (p. 65)

eres = are (one subject—permanent) (p. 138)

es = is (one subject—permanent) (pp. 60, 80, 138-9)

escribe = write (p. 80)

escuela = school (pp. 80-81)

España = Spain (p. 26)

español = Spanish (pp. 50, 138)

esquiar = to ski (p. 59)

está = is (one subject—changing) (pp. 59, 138)

estar = to be (changing) (Lesson 2 & p. 138)

estás = are (one subject—changing) (pp. 20, 138)

están = are (more than one subject—changing) (p. 138)

estilo = style (p. 95)

esto = this (p. 139)

estoy = I am...(changing) (pp. 20, 138)

estudiante(s) = student(s) (p. 85)

estudias = you study (informal) (p. 139)

estudio = I study (p. 139)

examen = exam (p. 117)

falda = skirt (p. 90)

falso = false (p. 105)

faltas = mistakes (p. 80)

familia = family (p. 50-51)

favorita/o = favorite (pp. 33, 61)

febrero = February (p. 60)

feliz = happy (p. 20)

fiesta = party (p. 100)

fresa = strawberry (p. 100)

GLOSARIO: SPANISH = ENGLISH

frijoles = beans (p. 45)

frío = cold (p. 70)

frutas = fruits (p. 100)

fútbol = soccer (p. 30)

fútbol americano = football (p. 30)

ganzo = goose (p. 22)

gata/o(s) = cat (female) (p. 50)

glosario = glossary (pp. 122-137)

gorra = cap (p. 90)

gracias = thank you (pp. 50, 139)

granjera/o = farmer (p. 22)

gris(es) = gray (p. 90)

guau, guau = bow-wow (p. 50)

gustar = to like (Lesson 3 & p. 138)

gusto = pleasure (p. 10)

hace = makes, does (one subject) (pp. 70, 138)

hacen = make, do (more than one) (p. 138)

hacer = to make (Lesson 7 & p. 138)

haces = makes, does (informal you) (p. 138)

hago = I do/make (pp. 70, 138)

hamburguesa = hamburger (p. 100)

hasta = until (see you) (p. 10)

hay = there is, there are (p. 15)

¡Hazlo! = Do it!
(pp. 17, 27, 37, 47, 57, 67, 77, 87, 97, 107)

helado = ice cream (p. 100)

hermana = sister (p. 50)

hermano = brother (p. 50)

hola = hello (p. 10)

hora = hour (time) (p. 139)

hoy = today (pp. 60, 70)

inglés = English (pp. 14, 24, 44, 54, 74, 84, 104)

¡Inténtalo! = Try it!
(pp. 12, 22, 32, 42, 52, 62, 72, 82, 92, 102)

igual = same, equal (p. 72)

ir = to go (Lesson 10 & pp. 80, 138)

¡Juégalo! = Play it!
(pp. 15, 25, 35, 45, 55, 65, 75, 85, 95, 105)

jueves = Thursday (p. 60)

juez = judge (p. 102)

junio = June (p. 60)

julio = July (p. 60)

la = the (pp. 50, 80, 90)

lápiz = pencil (p. 80)

las = the (pp. 80, 100)

lava = wash (p. 90)

¡Lávalos! = Wash them! (p. 91)

le gusta = one subject likes (p. 138)

leche = milk (p. 100)

GLOSARIO: SPANISH = ENGLISH

¡Léelo! = Read it!
(p. 13, 23, 33, 43, 53, 63, 73, 80, 83, 93, 103)

levanta = raise up / stand up (p. 80)

libro(s) = book(s) (pp. 34, 64, 80, 94)

líder = leader (p. 32)

listos = ready, smart (p. 30)

llamar = to be called/named (Lesson 1 & p. 138)

llena/o = full (p. 100)

llueve = it rains (p. 70)

lo = it (p. 80)

los = the (pp. 50, 80, 90)

lotería = lottery/bingo (p. 45)

luego = later (p. 10)

lunes = Monday (p. 60)

maestra/o(s) = teacher(s) female/male
(pp. 12, 21, 82)

mal = bad (pp. 20, 70)

mamá = mom (pp. 12, 50)

mañana = morning, tomorrow (p. 79)

mandatos = commands (p. 5, 121)

mano = hand (p. 80)

mapa = map (pp. 35, 80)

martes = Tuesday (p. 60)

más = more (pp. 40, 42)

matemáticas = math (p. 52)

mayo = May (p. 60)

marzo = March (p. 60)

Me llamo... =
My name is... / I am called... (pp. 10, 21, 138)

menos = less (pp. 40, 42)

mentira = lie (not true) (p. 105)

mesa = table (p. 80)

mi = my (p. 50, 59)

micrófono = microphone (p. 92)

miércoles = Wednesday (p. 60)

¡Míralo = Look at it!
(p. 16, 26, 36, 46, 56, 66, 76, 86, 96, 106)

mochila = backpack (p. 85)

moda = fashion (p. 92)

modelo = model (p. 92)

morada/o(s) = purple (p. 90)

muchas gracias =
thank you very much (p. 50)

mucha/o(s) = much, a lot, many (pp. 10, 40, 50)

Mucho gusto. = Nice to meet you. (p. 10)

mundo = world (p. 72)

muy = very (p. 20)

mi = my (pp. 50, 59)

miau = meow (p. 50)

mil = thousand (p. 60)

GLOSARIO: SPANISH = ENGLISH

nada = nothing (p. 50)

nadar = swim (p. 30)

negra/o(s) = black (p. 90)

nieva = it snows (p. 70)

nieve = snow (p. 70)

niña/o(s) = children/kids (pp. 8, 28, 32, 69, 115)

no = no (p. 12, 80, 100)

noche(s) = night(s) (p. 10, 100)

noventa = 90 ninety (p. 40)

noviembre = November (p. 60)

nueve = 9 nine (p. 40)

número(s) = number(s) (p. 40, 41, 52)

o = or (pp. 29, 40, 42, 61, 82, 105)

ochenta = 80 eighty (p. 40)

ocho = 8 eight (p. 40)

octubre = October (p. 60)

once = 11 eleven (p. 40)

otro/a(s) = other(s) (p. 93)

pantalones = pants (p. 90)

papá = dad (pp. 12, 50)

papas = potatoes (p. 100)

papel = paper (p. 80)

para = for, in order to, to (pp. 80, 100)

pares = pairs (p. 75)

Pásalo. = Pass it. (p. 92)

pato = duck (p. 22)

pedir = ask for, order (p. 80)

pegamento = glue (p. 80)

pequeña/o(s) = small (p. 69)

perdón = sorry, pardon (p. 15)

perro = dog (p. 50)

pobrecita/o(s) = poor little girl/boy (p. 20)

poca/o(s) = few, little (amount) (pp. 40, 70)

pollo = chicken (p. 100)

pon = put (one subject) (p. 55)

ponen = put (more than one subject) (p. 55)

por = for, because of, by, through (p. 50)

por favor = please (p. 50)

por qué = why (p. 139)

porque = because (p. 139)

postre = dessert (p. 100)

¡Practícalo! = Practice it! (p. 14, 24, 34, 44, 54, 64, 74, 84, 94, 104)

preguntas = questions (p. 139)

preparados = prepared (p. 30)

primaría = elementary/primary (p. 139)

qué = what (pp. 60, 70, 100, 139)

querer = to want (Lesson 8 & p. 138)

quién = who (p. 139)

GLOSARIO: SPANISH = ENGLISH

quiere = wants (one subject) (p. 138)

quieres = want (you—informal) (pp. 80, 138)

quieren = want (more than one subject) (p. 138)

quiero = I want, I love you (pp. 50, 80, 138)

quince = 15 fifteen (p. 40)

raya = row (p. 25)

roja/o(s) = red (p. 90)

¡Repítelo! = Repeat it!
(pp. 10, 20, 30, 40, 50, 60, 70, 80, 90, 100)

recorta = cut out (p. 80)

respuesta(s) = answer(s) (pp. 118-119)

ropa = clothing (pp. 90, 95)

rosa(s) = pink (p. 90)

sábado = Saturday (p. 60)

saca = take out (p. 80)

saludos = greetings (p. 20)

se llama = one subject is called/named (p. 138)

secreto = secret (p. 42)

secundaría = secondary / high school (p. 139)

seis = 6 six (p. 40)

señas = signs / sign language (p. 82)

ser = to be (permanent) (Lesson 6 & p. 138)

será = will be (p. 79)

sesenta = 60 sixty (p. 40)

setenta = 70 seventy (p. 40)

si = if (p. 82)

sí = yes (pp. 12, 71, 80)

siéntate = sit down (p. 80)

siesta = nap (p. 100)

siete = 7 seven (p. 40)

silla = chair (p. 80)

sol = sun (p. 70)

sólo = only (p. 70)

son = are
(for two or more—permanent) (pp. 112-113, 138)

soy = I am...(permanent) (p. 138)

suerte = luck (p. 62)

supermercado = supermarket / grocery store (p. 112)

tarea = homework
(pp. 19, 29, 39, 49, 59, 69, 79, 89, 99, 109)

tarde(s) = afternoon(s)/evening(s)/late (p. 10)

Te quiero. = I love you. (p. 50)

Te toca a ti. = It's your turn (p. 75)

te llamas = you are called/named (p. 10)

teléfono = telephone (p. 139)

tener = to have (Lesson 4 & p. 138)

tengo = I have (pp. 40, 138)

¡Termínalo! = Finish it!
(pp. 19, 29, 39, 49, 59, 69, 79, 89, 99, 109)

tienda = store (p. 99)

tiene = has (one subject) (pp. 59, 113, 138)

GLOSARIO: SPANISH = ENGLISH

tienen = have (more than one subject) (p. 138)

¿Tienes...? = Do you have...? (p. 40)

tienes = have (informal you) (pp. 40, 138)

tijeras = scissors (p. 80)

tiras = throw, roll (the dice) (p. 62)

todo = everything (p. 55)

todos = everyone (p. 55)

toma = take (p. 55)

tomar = to take (p. 100)

traje de baño = swimsuit (p. 90)

trece = 13 thirteen (p. 40)

treinta = 30 thirty (p. 40)

tres = 3 three (pp. 25, 40)

triste = sad (p. 20)

tú = you (informal) (pp. 20, 50)

tu(s) = your (informal) (p. 42, 52, 60, 139)

turistas = tourists (p. 35)

un(a) = a (pp. 30, 70)

uno = 1 one (p. 40)

unos(as) = some (p. 70)

usa = use (p. 80)

usted(es) = you (formal) (p. 138)

va = goes (one subject) (p. 138)

vacaciones = vacation (p. 80)

van = go (more than one subject) (p. 138)

vas = go (you—informal) (pp. 100, 138)

¡Vámonos! = Let's go! (p. 50)

ve = sees (one subject) (p. 138)

veinte = 20 twenty (p. 40)

ven = see (more than one subject) (p. 138)

veo = I see (p. 90)

ver = to see (Lesson 9 & p. 138)

verbos = verbs (table) (p. 138)

verdad = truth (p. 105)

verde(s) = green (p. 90)

verduras = vegetables (p. 100)

ves = see (you—informal) (p. 90)

viajar = to travel (p. 59)

viento = windy (p. 70)

viernes = Friday (p. 60)

violeta(s) = violet (p. 90)

visitar = visit (p. 35)

voy = I go (pp. 100, 138)

y = and (p. 20)

ya = already, now (p. 30)

yo = I (pp. 41, 50, 80, 90, 100)

Yo digo... = I say... (p. 50)

yogur = yogurt (p. 100)

zapatos = shoes (p. 90)

INFINITIVE FORM TO...	I = YO FORM PRESENT TENSE		ONE SUBJECT = ELLA, ÉL, USTED FORM PRESENT TENSE		YOU PLURAL/ THEY = USTEDES/ELLOS FORM PRESENT TENSE	
	SPANISH	ENGLISH	SPANISH	ENGLISH	SPANISH	ENGLISH
1. LLAMAR	yo me llamo	I am called (my name is)	él se llama	he is called (his name is)	ellos se llaman	they are called (their names are)
2. ESTAR	yo estoy	I am (changing)	María está	Mary is (changing)	Mateo, Celeste, Abrahán, Manolo y Amalia están	Matt, Shannon, Abraham, Nolan and Amelia are
3. GUSTAR	A mí me gusta	I like	usted le gusta	you like	Catalina, Mateo y Emilia les gustan	Sharre, Matt and Emily like
4. TENER	yo tengo	I have	él tiene	he has	Diego, Cintia, Tomás y Miguel tienen	Cindy, Tom & Michael have
5. DECIR	yo digo	I say	Francisco dice	Francis says	Carina y Andres dicen	Carrie and Andrew say
6. SER	yo soy	I am (permanent)	Diego es	Doug is (permanent)	ustedes son	you all are
7. HACER	yo hago	I do, I make	Araceli hace	Arvaleen does, makes	Santiago y Rosa hacen	James and Rose do, make
8. QUERER	yo quiero	I want	ella quiere	she wants	ustedes quieren	you all want
9. VER	yo veo	I see	usted ve	you see	Natalia y Eliana ven	Natalie and Eliana see
10. IR	yo voy	I go	él va	he goes	Melchor y Carolina van	Merle and Carolyn go
COMER	yo como	I eat	usted come	you eat	ustedes comen	you all eat

¿PREGUNTAS? = QUESTIONS?

¿QUIÉN? = WHO?
¿Quién es? = Who is it?

¿CUÁL? = WHAT?
¿Cuál es tu número de teléfono? = What is your phone number?

¿Cuál es tu dirección? = What is your address?

¿Cuál es tu escuela, primaría o secundaría? = What or which one is your school, primary or secondary?

¿QUÉ? = WHAT?
Use when the answer is a specific item.

¿Qué hora es? = What time is it?

¿Qué es esto? = What is this?

¿CÓMO? = WHAT?
How or what did you just say?

¿Cómo te llamas? = What is your name? (How are you called?)

¿Cómo estás? = How are you?

¿Cómo dices _____ en español? = How do you say _____ in Spanish?

¿DÓNDE? = WHERE?
¿De dónde eres? = Where are you from?

Soy de _____. (Place of birth) = I'm from _____.

¿CUÁNDO? = WHEN?
¿Cuándo es tu cumpleaños? = When is your birthday?

¿POR QUÉ? = WHY?
¿Por qué estudias español? = Why do you study Spanish?

PORQUE = BECAUSE
Estudio español porque quiero hablar con mis amigos. = I study Spanish because I want to talk with my friends.

HOW MUCH/MANY? = ¿CUÁNTO/CUÁNTA?
¿Cuánto más para hacer? = How much more to do?

¿Cuántos años tienes _____? = How old is _____?

WANT TO LEARN SPANISH OR ENGLISH?

Would you like to order more books for coworkers, friends or family?
Here is how: Order online at SpanishChatCompany.com

ONLINE GAMES, FLASHCARDS, ACTIVITIES & VIDEOS

SPANISHCHATCOMPANY.COM

MINI CHATBOOKS

www.ingramcontent.com/pod-product-compliance
Lightning Source LLC
Chambersburg PA
CBHW081217230426
43666CB00015B/2764